DIVORCE

MAKING IT WORK BETTER

DIVORCE

MAKING IT WORK BETTER

JOHN BROWNRIGG

First published as an ebook in 2013 by the Hornbeam Press,
45 Falkland Road, London NW5 2XB

All names in the case examples have been changed.

Hornbeam Press
45 Falkland Road
London
NW5 2XB
hornbeampress@aol.com

ISBN 978 0956523 679

British Library Cataloguing in Publication Data.
A catalogue record for this book is available from the British Library.

Typeset by Troubador Publishing Ltd
Printed and bound in the UK by TJ International, Padstow, Cornwall

Contents

This book is dedicated to the troubled children of parents who could not discover a constructive way through separation.

I am very grateful to five people whose encouragement and ability enabled the highly unlikely to happen: John Brownrigg writing a book on his approach to divorce law. They are Emma Dally, Jane Walker, Julie Sheppard, Caroline Fell, and above all Richard Ehrlich, whose capacity to interpret and ability to deliver as an editor have been remarkable.

Introduction

I have been divorced over 100 times a year for the last 30 years. But only in a professional capacity, thank goodness. I am a divorce lawyer, and seeing several thousand people go through this painful process has given me a great deal of experience both of the process and of its human costs.

But I have also learned of the positive aspects. Divorce is never anything other than painful and difficult, but there are ways of lessening the pain. This book aims to explain how to do that, and to help you find your own way through with a minimum of suffering, conflict, and expense.

This is not a book about the law, though obviously the law plays an important part in it. It is not about legal statutes or dramatic cases fought by the super-rich. It is about how you can work towards finding your own solutions to your own problems on separation or divorce, even when you cannot see a way through the unknown. It is about giving you an opportunity to understand, control, and manage a major change in your life.

I feel a responsibility to educate and inform from my experience as a matrimonial lawyer and mediator, in the hope that better decisions can be made by separating couples who need to keep their head through one of the most stressful times of their life. It is always said that divorce is the second most difficult grieving event after the death of a loved one, with moving house in third place behind those two. When you think that divorce often requires one or both partners to move house, you can imagine just how devastating an effect it is likely to have. And its effects are long-lasting. Matrimonial fallout doesn't just involve the separating couple. It has a profound effect on the whole family, and especially on children. We all know children who have been unable to maintain communication with one or both parents when there has been conflict surrounding divorce. The family can be fractured if there is no attempt to work together at the time of separation. If you don't put a plaster cast on that fracture immediately, it will never mend. The fracture isn't caused by the divorce in itself. It is caused by the impact of conflict. And the fracture can repeat itself down the generations.

I hope that this book may help you avoid that fracture, to minimise conflict by taking control of your divorce. Do not behave in a way that removes your partner from your children's lives. Do not behave in a way that will make your children see your partner in a bad light. Do not put your children in the middle of the conflict between the two of you, which means that your children feel they have to end up parenting their parents. Children almost always try to protect the parent whom they perceive to be weaker in the relationship and separation, or the parent whom they share their day-to-day life with. Whatever the details may be, it is unfair on your children and ultimately destructive for you, too.

And it is all avoidable, if you resolve to behave like grownups and carry through with your resolution.

- Fact: Over 30 per cent of first marriages break down
- Fact: Over 40 per cent of second and subsequent marriages break down
- Fact: The majority of cohabiting relationships break down
- Fact: Over one in every three children come from separated families

If you are going to join their number, I hope that this book will help make the process less bad for you and more constructive for your family. I have written it because I've seen so much of the destruction that comes out of divorces conducted through conflict.

My focus has always been on constructive negotiation and mediation, rather than litigation and issuing proceedings through the courts. From the beginning, this approach to family law seemed to be different from my peers.

I always liked the idea of lawyers and clients meeting together in a room. I always liked the idea of discussing matters by telephone. I never understood the need for lawyers to posture in negotiations, write reams of paper, and issue proceedings that were not worth the money they cost. It always struck me that discussion could cut through misunderstanding.

I have also believed for many decades that people are generally well intentioned and trying to do the best they can in difficult circumstances. I therefore have been slow to be sceptical of people's motives.

As a family lawyer, I am proud to say that only a very small percentage of my cases go to court. I would estimate that the percentage of my clients who issue proceedings to deal with the finances each year is well below 3 per cent of my caseload, substantially lower than that of my peers who have been keener to issue proceedings through the courts at an early stage when dealing with similar cases. Of course, I also recognise that some cases demand action through the courts because the two parties are not both prepared to come to the table and discuss matters.

At first, when I was pressing for meetings and discussions, particularly with clients present, a very small proportion of lawyers would take up my offer. They were more comfortable in taking a position on paper after having detailed discussions with their client, and trying to achieve for their client the very best outcome, regardless of its impact down the line.

Now the situation has evolved, and increasingly large

numbers of lawyers are prepared to meet and talk, not just outside of a courtroom. They still do like to control the preconditions to any meeting, rather than allow a free-flowing discussion. But their attitudes have changed in ways that I think are much better.

I do not believe my clients have missed out or done worse as a result of my attempts to work cooperatively rather than antagonistically. Indeed, I believe they have done better. I believe their families have benefitted. I believe their children have benefitted. I also believe that my clients' self-confidence has grown, and that they have become empowered in the process of divorce.

The Most Important Checklist: Ten things not to do

You will see much more about these points in the pages of this book, but it is worth starting out with them because they are the most important things to bear in mind when trying to work through the divorce process. Remember them at all times from the moment when you are first considering whether to divorce.

Do not:

1. Be violent or abusive
2. Stop parenting
3. Lose control
4. Over-depend on children
5. Underestimate what the kids know
6. Stop supporting your partner
7. Stop acknowledging your partner's positives
8. Stop listening
9. Be part of the conflict
10. Over-support financially, creating unreasonable expectations and long-term financial difficulty

CHAPTER ONE

Into the Unknown

We all have friends who have separated or divorced. We all have family members who are separated or divorced. We have all witnessed the experience of separating couples and the pain it causes. We know children of separated or divorced parents, and have seen their pain (often concealed) in a situation that is beyond their control.

Yet despite this direct knowledge that we all have of divorce and separation, things are completely different when it comes to understanding it when we have to deal with it in our own lives. We can look at it fairly objectively in others, but the hurt we experience when it concerns us directly makes that impossible. Perhaps we are just not emotionally ready to apply the same objectivity to ourselves. Whatever the explanation, we have terrible difficulty understanding the causes and the impact of separation on ourselves, our partner, and our children.

If you are thinking about divorce or separation, or you have been confronted with that prospect, it helps to understand the process, and to look at the events leading to separation from more than just your own perspective. The more you understand, the better you can achieve a balance of power in negotiations and a knowledge of the options available. This should help you to do much of the process yourself, and that in turn will free you to focus on the areas where you need advice, and to seek that advice from the relevant professionals and bodies.

Why do marriages fail?

Marriages fail for a number of reasons, but in my experience certain problems crop up again and again, and these are the ones you need to watch for. Some of the most serious and most common of those I encounter:

- Lack of communication
- Financial problems
- Affairs
- Lack of respect
- A stonewalled response to criticism or conversation
- Open criticism of you to your friends and relatives
- Refusal to go to counselling
- Your partner has an unhealthy relationship with a third party

If you see these signs, then this is the time to consider counselling. You need to put energy into your relationship in an attempt to sort out the problem.

Communication problems

Poor communication is the most common warning sign of a broken relationship. This can lead to losing touch with what is important in your relationship. It can lead to personal attacks, lack of respect and a refusal to look for the positive in yourself, your partner and the family.

Often, people think that communication is about talking, but true communication starts with listening. Listening leads to understanding what someone is trying to say and can often prevent more serious problems down the line. There are certain practical steps you can take to prevent a crisis in communication between you and your partner.

Get better at communicating. If you think you have been misunderstood, try explaining yourself further. You can only do this, however, if you respect your partner's opinion and wish to try and encourage them to respect your opinion. Communication takes time. As in the real world, whether in our mundane daily dealings or at the highest of political levels, where there has been conflict it is important to be quick to forgive and to look forward, positively and constructively.

Stay civil and respectful. It goes without saying that it cannot help to talk to your partner in a rude or disdainful way, or to criticise your partner in front of others. This is the case not only with your children but with extended family and friends. All that happens if you talk to your partner in a rude or disdainful way, or if you are critical of your partner in front of family and friends, is that you alienate some of them. You may think you are getting support for your criticism and for trying to have a positive impact on your partner's behaviour, but you're not. You are only making matters worse through expressing yourself openly, rather than trying to resolve matters direct with your partner, or with the help of professionals such as counsellors.

Don't personalise every disagreement, or interpret disagreement as an attack on you as an individual. Just because somebody disagrees with you, it does not mean to say that they reject your views in general, or you as a person or as their partner.

Be extra cautious with your children. It is particularly important not to criticise your partner in front of your children, however wronged you may feel. Whatever their age, your children look to their parents to be an example – even (and perhaps more than ever) through marriage breakdown. They love you both and they look to you for a guide as to the way ahead. They look to you not to surround them in parental conflict.

Remember: your marriage difficulties and breakdown arise out of your decisions, not theirs. They do not need to be involved in your conflict. Nor should they be asked directly or indirectly to take sides or sympathise with one of you to the exclusion of the other.

Think about what you do, and be responsible for your own actions. Be slow to over-react and try to be constructive – you have a co-parenting relationship to protect after all.

Financial problems

Financial problems can bind people together, if the united effort needed to solve them gives a couple a common cause and sense of shared responsibility. But they are frequently the subject of disagreement in a relationship because financial planning – and financial anxiety – is omnipresent. Most of us have money worries and are concerned about our financial position much of the time. This is quite natural in that we all aspire to provide as much as we can for our families. And these anxieties become even more prominent when a couple is about to separate.

When two adults get married, they may bring into the marriage widely different attitudes towards money learned in their youth. It is incredibly difficult to change those attitudes. If the couple have strongly differing views, that can inevitably lead to conflict. So it is back to communication – listening and exchanging views, and looking at how family money will be controlled together and the responsibility shared.

Find your own combined way of dealing with family finances that work for you both as individuals and for the family as a whole.

Affairs

Many would regard it as strange how some people risk their marriage for the sake of an extramarital affair, but those relationships are usually a sign of other problems of communication. They say it takes three to commit adultery, and just because one half of a partnership has an affair it does not mean that the other has no responsibility for the situation arising. Something is normally wrong with the marriage.

Needless to say, I am not denying or downplaying the wounded feelings of the partner who has been betrayed. They feel humiliated, and rejected. And these feelings are made all the more bitter by fears about sexually transmitted diseases, which their partner may have picked up in the course of their affair. If the affair was a casual fling with a stranger, those fears may be even more acute.

It is not inevitable that couples split up after an affair. Staying together is an option, and counsellors can be of enormous value in helping deal with this problem. They can also help deal with the problems leading to the affair.

Extramarital affairs often have a long build-up – they don't happen without at least some deliberation and confusion. If you find that you are looking to have a relationship outside your marriage, or even if you feel you are simply open to the idea, pause and ask yourself whether there is a problem in your relationship with your spouse. On marriage your relationship was intended to be monogamous, and if one of you is susceptible to a third party, then they are unhappy with the marriage in some form or other. If you are unable to talk to your partner about this, give serious thought to the idea of seeing a counsellor. If you can address those desires before they become reality, you will have a better chance of improving your relationship – and of avoiding its total breakdown.

Commitment to the marriage

If you find yourself losing your commitment to the marriage, then try and find it afresh. For example, if you work excessively away from home because you feel you need to provide for the family, consider if it is really in the family's best interests. Commitment takes time, energy, focus and the capacity to recognise when you need to do more – for example, at the time of a family bereavement, loss of employment, or an enforced house move. Be aware of what losing the marriage and separation look like before continuing to plough your own furrow.

This is especially important if your partner is asking you to change or expressing unhappiness with some aspect of your behaviour. A common example of this is when one partner has chosen to work abroad for substantial amounts of time, or to work long, punishing hours because he or she thinks this is 'good for the family.' If you fit into that category, you are acting out of good motives: you want to provide as well as possible for your family. But do not assume that your partner wants that extra income above all. What they really want is you: your presence, your commitment, your involvement with the children, your full participation in family life. They are willing you to change, and you owe it to everyone – yourself included – to listen to them. You're putting your career and your boss over your family.

Of course, this situation can be reversed. Sometimes it is the earning partner who wants his or her partner to work part-time, in the belief that work outside the home would bring in extra money and take financial pressure off the whole family. Perhaps the children have gone to school so the non-working partner has more time. Sharing paid work, just as they share parenting, can enable both partners to play a full role in family life.

Whatever the facts of your situation, do not assume that you have all the answers. Pay attention to all the things that are going on around you within your family. Listen to others. And especially to your partner.

Jealousy

Jealousy is a very common cause of separation and divorce, and it often springs from a change in your pattern of living. So, if your relationship passed through the first blush of romance and you are not thinking that you have made an instant mistake, often the first time of difficulty is on the birth of the first child. Fathers often – perhaps always – feel jealous with regard to the mother's shift in affection to their child. They resent the time and commitment that that child receives from the mother, which they perceive to be at their loss. In addition, they may feel threatened by the close physical bond between the child and the mother, however natural it may be.

The spring point for jealousy can come much later, for instance when the children go to school or nursery and the mother returns to work. Often the father feels jealous of his wife's new-found independence, socially and financially, and has difficulty in adjusting to not being depended on in his role of provider to the family.

Over and above instances of affairs and parents waiting 'for their children to grow up', before getting divorced, another frequent pressure point comes on retirement. The life-changing prospect of sharing not only weekends and holidays but each day in the constant presence of the partner can prove a threat. Some couples cannot work through this. Couples of this age also often have access to greater financial resources and are less concerned by the financial constraints of divorce.

Be aware of these issues. Take stock and work on them, and indeed plan for them. If you cannot work on them effectively enough, then do not hesitate to involve counsellors and to give time to an improvement in your relationship.

Thinking about leaving…

Very often one partner in a marriage knows for six to twelve months that they are considering separation and divorce. They try not to rush into things and try to understand the implications of the decision for themselves and for their children. Instead of publicising their thoughts, sharing their thoughts, or going to counselling, they work out in detail the impact on their own life of separation – the pros and the cons.

They work out the best scenario and the worst scenario. They secure in their mind with whom the children will be living and how good arrangements can be made for the children. They look at the financial implications and their capacity to survive. They look at where they will live, where the children will go to school, and what they will live off. In their own way they are going through their own grieving process, their feelings of denial, fear, adaptation, loneliness, friendship, guilt, rejection, grief and anger. They want to see their way clear to letting go and regaining a feeling of self-worth.

When they are through those processes, they get themselves into a position where they feel able, one way or another, to communicate their decision to their partner. For some reason, however unrealistic, they also persuade themselves that their partner will be able to adjust to their view swiftly and expect the partner to deal with the situation effortlessly.

The shocking news

So what of the partner who will be 'on the receiving end'? More often than not, they are oblivious to their partner's thought processes over the past year. This is not a surprise because often it has been kept secret from them as a defence mechanism by their partner. They find it hard to believe the position that they are in, and find it is often too late to salvage a joint commitment to the marriage. They start their own grieving process, but six months to a year behind and with a different agenda. While one is in denial, the other has already let go and is enjoying the prospect of an alternative way of life that they feel has become available to them.

Sometimes the relationship can be salvaged at this point. But it takes enormous effort because of the distance between the two partners' agendas, and because one person is six to twelve months behind the thinking of the other. That partner is running to catch up with their partner and trying to slow them down from what they consider to be over-impulsive and incisive action.

Catching the moment

The news that your partner is considering separation and divorce is always a terrible thing to hear. But it is possible to do something that I call 'catching the moment', and when it is successful it really can make separation work better.

Catching the moment means opening up to your partner rather than keeping your thoughts, fears and plans secret. It should be done early – the earlier the better. The aim is to really think hard about certain vital questions and get a sense of what it will be like to face them in reality, not just in your plans and dreams. Points such as:

- Your doubts about your relationship
- Can the marriage be salvaged?
- What separation would be like for you, your partner, and your children
- What are your options?
- Which are the options that each of you prefer?

If you are the one planning to leave, get all of this out there as early as possible. Prepare your partner for separation, and consider getting counselling either on your own or together.

When I am going through these options with a couple that has come to me for mediation, I always use a flipchart to explore things. There the options on both sides can be written down and looked at in a full list, and clients invariably find this very useful. You might want to use the technique with your partner, even if you don't see a counsellor or lawyer or mediator to start with.

The children

Catching the moment also means that both partners have to focus on co-parenting as well as each other. If the person driving the separation can slow down slightly and involve the partner, that will help the partner adjust to their thought process. And then it may be, even if they cannot commit themselves to each other, that they can at least at an early stage commit themselves to co-parenting their children and working together for the children.

It is difficult for a parent, thinking as a parent, to make a bad decision for a child. It is all too easy to make a bad decision for a child if you are thinking as an individual, and acting solely or principally in your own self-interest.

Take an example such as a summer holiday. You have agreed the dates for the holiday and how the children will share their time. Dates and tickets have been booked for the children to visit your extended family in Cornwall, and a deposit has been paid for a stay at a holiday club.

At the very last moment, the opportunity arises for a fabulous break for your children and your former partner which will take them to your in-laws' holiday home in Scotland. All their cousins on your former partner's side will be there. You know the children would hate to miss it – but the downside is that it will mess up your plans.

If you are able to adapt, do it. As a parent, consider how important it is to stick to your plans – and how important it is to show flexibility. Speaking as an individual, you might think that 'No, it's too late to change these plans – we've decided.' Or: 'This isn't fair to me or my parents.' But your children may be more flexible than that. And the long-term gain from showing flexibility will almost certainly be greater than the gain of sticking to your plans simply because they have been made.

This is not to criticise you for wanting to stick to the plans, and to get your full allotted time with your children. Naturally parents want their children to be with them on special days and special times of year, and they can easily start thinking of their right as an individual to have that company.

This is their first mistake.

Parents have no rights in this situation, they only have responsibilities. The only people in the family who have rights are the children. The children probably do not mind which side of the family they spend their holiday with. Even if they do have preferences, what they really want – however old they are – is to have no conflict between their parents. If the parents think as individuals, it is highly unlikely that they will be able to give their children a clear guide as to how they should spend their time over the holiday period. If, however, the parents think together as parents working together for the children, it is very often possible for an imaginative, positive, constructive way forward to be found, avoiding conflict.

Case example: Jayne and Anthony

Jayne and Anthony and their two children Caroline and Carlos have had regular patterns of contact over the Christmas festive period: they have alternated Christmas and New Year for the past four years. This year was the turn when the children would share time with Jayne and her new family at her home in Bristol over the Christmas period. As it happened, however, Anthony had extended family coming over from Canada and Australia to share Christmas and to celebrate his mother's 60th birthday at his home in London.

Jayne had been very excited at the thought of having Caroline and Carlos for Christmas and made all sorts of plans, including going to the pantomime, carol services and meeting her new partner's extended family. She was tempted to insist on sticking to the old established pattern of contact and insisting that the children stay with her until they go to Anthony for New Year. But of course Anthony was very keen for his extended family from Canada and Australia to meet with his children, especially because of his mother's 60th birthday.

The children did not mind. They do not know Anthony's relatives from Canada or Australia particularly well, and do not place much store by their grandmother's 60th birthday. They simply needed a clear lead from their parents.

Jayne and Anthony worked out a solution together, thinking as parents and not as individuals. They agreed to change the usual pattern of contact so that the children stayed with Jayne until 11a.m. on Christmas Day. That way they could wake up there and have presents with Jayne and her new family. Then Anthony collected them in Bristol and drove them back to London to a late Christmas lunch with the extended family. The children stayed until 28th December, before returning to be with Jayne for New Year.

Cooperating in this way can show parents that they both have a future, even if they cannot live together. They may learn that if they go through the process without conflict, they should be able to help the children cope with their separation better by giving their children a combined, clear lead and financial stability.

Counselling: an invaluable tool

It is very dangerous for couples to get stuck in conflict with completely different agendas. They end up forcing each other into positions that they do not wish to take, and forgetting about the needs of the children. It is vital to be positive, constructive and forward-looking through the pain, and frequently it is appropriate to consider individual counselling or co-counselling at this time to help catalyse working towards the co-parenting imperative. The benefits of counselling can take so many forms, including:

- Empowering one of the parties, or indeed both of the parties
- Ensuring each parent listens to the other
- Reassuring a parent that they are not mad, that what they are thinking is normal
- Explaining the stress and supporting each parent
- Encouraging parents to learn how to live apart, but parent together
- Identify whether reconciliation really is a possibility
- Identify if the parents can reconnect as a couple, or if the parents can reconnect as parents
- Anger counselling
- Practical strategies for survival on a day-to-day basis
- Practical strategies for delaying the implementation of decisions that have been made for health reasons or other reasons

If you are considering leaving your marriage, or even if you have made up your mind to do so, counselling can improve the quality of all your decision-making. It is worth doing, and the sooner you do it the more you will benefit from it.

CHAPTER TWO

Whom Can You Trust?

If you find yourself confronting divorce or separation, you really need to work out whom you can turn to, and whom you can trust. You are looking for a direction. If you rush off in a certain direction on impulse, or follow the first advice you receive, you could find yourself going completely wrong. It's like driving towards oncoming traffic in the wrong lane of a motorway.

Before turning to anyone for advice or guidance, you need to make sure that you know (A) where you are trying to get to and (B) how you are going to get there. Do not let yourself be drawn into taking action without knowing both those things. If you intend to separate, be sure – completely sure – that it is what you want to do. If you are doing something just because somebody (or your own inner voice) told you to follow your instincts, and start taking action, you may find yourself heading down a path that turns out to be irreversible.

Case example: Louise and John

Louise has not been happy in her family life for some time. John has been working too hard and not giving her enough attention, focussing instead on career advancement. There are two children who have just started junior school, and they are the apple of both Louise's and John's eye. Louise has a flirtatious fling with an old flame which is physical and not meaningful. John's very swift reaction – decided upon with barely any pause for reflection – is to blame Louise and move out to live with his parents in the short term. Louise finds that she can cope quite well without John and it's harder for John to return than he thought it should be because he put all of the blame on Louisa. If he had listened to the problems in the marriage and shared responsibility, and talked things through rather than run away, he wouldn't have taken a potentially irreversible step by removing himself from the home.

Your one safe bet

The first person to trust is the parent in you. As a parent, you should ask: 'what is the right thing for me to do?' If you ask yourself, 'what do I want to do about separating?', you may get a very different answer to the question if you ask yourself as a parent what is the right thing to do.

I often preface my questions to clients by asking them what they think is the best way forward 'as a parent'. This is because brains are funny things – wired and fired in different ways. I believe I get different answers from a person if I ask them what they think 'as a parent', because I believe they are using a different part of their brain in providing me with the answer. I am therefore trying to fire the wires in the brain that lead to responsible parental decisions, rather than potentially selfish individual decisions.

This is just a personal theory of mine and may or may not be true, but the results don't lie. People think differently when they are thinking as a parent – and I think they think more clearly and in a more considered way. Your quality of judgement as a parent and quality of the decisions that you make as a parent will far exceed the quality of the decisions you make as an individual going through the grieving process.

Your partner?

Do not write off trusting your partner. Look to their motivation as a parent, and look to them as someone with whom your relationship is changing. The two of you are becoming parents, as opposed to soul-mates, but remember: you have trusted their judgement in the past, and have shared positive, constructive and good times. Those positives can continue working for you in your new relationship if you put them to work together.

Recognise that you both need time, often different amounts of it, for grieving. But do not get stuck in non-communication. Work at communicating through your grief, and if necessary do not hesitate to involve counsellors.

Your children?

Can you trust your children? Much will depend on their age, but we all know that children have great clarity of vision, not least because they have been less conditioned by the years to have standard responses to potential conflict. Parents, by contrast, carry a lot of pre-conditioning and are influenced by their past and by those around them in their reaction to conflict. However, it is extremely dangerous to involve children in your relationship difficulties. Remember:

- No child wants to hear one biological parent criticised by the other parent
- No child wants to be forced to take sides
- No child should be put in a position of parenting their parent
- No child should be put in a position of having to tell their parent what he or she wants to hear

Children are too vulnerable to your persuasion, and too open and willing in their wish to protect you. They may also be feeling guilty and blame themselves for their parents' separation.

It is vital that you listen to your children and hear what they say, but you do not have to press them for their views or use them as a sounding board. Indeed, it is important not to over-involve them or lean on them, however much you need someone to communicate to who is supportive and/or passive in your relationship problems.

So, for example, if there is a clash of interests over a weekend where one parent wishes the children to be with them to go to a family wedding, and the other parent also wishes the children to be with them for another family wedding, the children look to the parents to resolve that issue without conflict and to give them a clear lead.

Put more simply: if I were to ask one parent, 'Do you want to have the children on Christmas Eve and then take them to your brother for Christmas lunch?', that parent would say 'Yes'. If I ask the other parent the same question, that parent would say 'Yes'.

However, if I ask both parents, 'What do you think as a parent is the best way for the children to share time over Christmas Eve and Christmas lunch?' I would probably receive a different answer.

Parents?

By definition, your parents are normally partial and supportive of you, so they are a natural person to turn to. But they are not necessarily the right people from whom to take advice. They have their own agenda and their own role, often as a grandparent. They seek to empower their child who is weak, vulnerable and in a difficult place, and are often deeply depended upon for practical, physical as well as emotional assistance. As parents, they want the best for their child. They want to look after their child. They are partial, as all parents are, and love you, their child, unconditionally. They want to appear to do whatever they can to support you.

For example, parents may help out with transport, child care and money. They may believe that as a consequence they have a valid viewpoint as to how the new situation should be handled. Because they like the power and because they like the role of helping their child (you) look after their grandchild, they are often very happy taking over the role that before was covered by your partner. They may be angry with your partner and want to hurt them. They might like the idea of supporting you in proving to your partner that you are self-sufficient and don't need your partner who has rejected you.

That, however, overlooks your children's needs. It also takes away power from your partner and transfers it to your parents. They might like to try and perpetuate that role because they enjoy it. You need to be careful that they do not misinterpret their behaviour and your additional needs by bad-mouthing the 'lack of interest' shown by your partner. Your parents may know little of the objective background to the breakdown of the relationship.

It is important for your parents' additional help to be, as far as possible, unconditional and uncritical of your partner's contributions. They should also promote and be positive about your partner, even if it is the case that your partner has left their child (you).

It is not difficult for your parents to persuade you that their support of you is completely rational, but they are not impartial and they may not have the life skills to help you make the best decisions, through a time of grieving, as a parent yourself. Try to distance the practical, physical and emotional support on which you depend from the guidance you seek and the advice you may be given. It is difficult as a parent to be objective.

Case example: Bill and Gemma

Bill and Gemma had had a regular routine sharing the collection and return of their children, Joe and Alice, from their two schools. Bill had left the family home at Gemma's request and moved to his parents' home 15 miles away. It was no longer practical for Bill to do the collection and return as he had done under the old routine. Gemma had work commitments and her parents stepped into the void. Bill therefore collected the children for an evening visit at 5p.m. from the home of Gemma's parents, Peter and Di, and not from school.

Peter and Di used their time with the children to praise Gemma and be quietly critical of Bill, whose new situation made it necessary for them to step into the breach. And when Bill called to collect Alice and Joe, Peter and Di made their feelings known. Alice and Jo not only heard but clearly understood the growing animosity between their father and their grandparents. This put them in a difficult position and made them uncertain of whom to support and how.

Friends?

Your friends are always supportive and always willing to give advice. Normally they are there to offer help. They have come across other people who have separated and divorced, and they may have useful experience to share with you.

But beware. Friends are people to whom you can vent your feelings and have confidence in their support, but even though they are sincerely trying to help they can make matters worse. They are not always objective. They can be easily influenced by your tone, your exaggeration, and your need for sympathy and support. They may hear stories, distorted through a 'Chinese Whisper' across a community. They may choose to communicate with one of the parties, not both. You need a listening ear, not directive advice. You want someone who is able to listen but does not feel the need to repeat what they've heard, especially to your partner or your partner's friends and family.

Friends often think they have to choose between the members of the couple as to whom they will support. They can get caught up in one person's story. Old commitments can lead to unconditional partial support. Friends often only have one side of the story and a personal agenda. Be very wary of them, even if they are siding with you and critical of your partner.

The press?

What we read, what we see on television and hear on the radio, is designed to attract our interest. The press focus on the negative, and on celebrity conflict and big-money cases which make a good newsworthy story. A good divorce is not a sexy subject for a tabloid. Many of the press stories relate to stories provided by people trying to get their partial point across. It is self-promotion from the individuals involved in conflict, trying to gain favour.

The same can be said of the political approach where politicians formulate a policy and extend views designed in their own self-interest to attract support, regardless of the potential for reduction of conflict through separation and divorce. Why else is there still the need in this country for there to be fault-based divorce if you wish to be divorced in a time period of less than two years?

The press does not print stories about fine examples of divorce; if they did, the stories would not make good copy. You do not have to try to imitate sensational approaches of wealthy celebrities. Even if you have (or think you have) the money to wage these battles, they are a bad place to go.

Counsellors?

Counsellors are a listening ear. They can be a catalyst to adaptation to change. They can become the voice of the children, and they are experienced in helping two parents reduce conflict and promote co-parenting. They also know how to help empower individuals who are being manipulated by their partners. They have a genuine interest in supporting people and know how to be objective at all times, while at the same time being conscious of dropping off their own agendas when dealing with relationship issues. This helps because their skills enable them to help individuals and couples without prejudging them, and help individuals and couples find their own way forward to better solutions. Choose a counsellor after doing research to make sure they are the right person for you.

Lawyers?

Many people think you need a lawyer as you enter into the unknown. They are not always wrong. There are even some circumstances when you need protecting while you do nothing. Using a lawyer's advice will help give you a chance to think things through and decide how you want to proceed. A good lawyer should be able to hold you in a protective bubble while you work things out without feeling the need to make decisions hastily.

But you should tread carefully with lawyers until you have worked out what it is you are trying to achieve. Many lawyers think that their job is to do the best for their client. That can mean getting the best financial outcome, or endorsing the client's every wish, and trying to satisfy the client's needs at any given time, even if the client is behaving unusually through a grieving process and has difficulty in taking a step back. If you are going through an emotional time, and you get an impression from your lawyer that he or she is planning to squeeze every penny he can from your partner and take them to the cleaners, it may be just the short-term music to your ears that you wanted to hear. But for the long term it may be the basis of a cacophony of pain and misery that follows.

You may find it difficult to deal with lawyers because they can by nature be controlling and directive. They can use language that is not familiar to you or your partner. They can be more focused on outcome and closed to resolution. They may have a view as to what financial settlement you should achieve or how your children's time should be shared between you and your partner.

It may be impossible to resolve matters by agreement on the basis of the lawyer's view of best outcome. The existence of an agreement between you and your partner may be more important than sticking rigidly to your guns. Follow your own personal agenda, not your lawyer's. The lawyer to rely on is a lawyer whom you have met, whose attitude you approve of, who is accessible, and who you believe has the family's interests at heart, as well as your own. Find a lawyer who listens as well as advises, and who focuses on the big picture – even if some of what he or she says differs from your own view. There is much more about choosing – and dealing with – your lawyer in the next chapter.

CHAPTER THREE

Choosing Your Lawyer

Choosing the right lawyer for you is, as I hardly need to say, vitally important. But how do you find that lawyer when your state of mind is so confused at a heightened time of grieving and uncertainty? Check them out on their website and in legal directories. Find out about their expertise and qualifications, and ask around – in that order. And remember: just because one lawyer was right for your friend, he or she may not be right for you if you want to do things differently. Look for someone who:

- Does what you ask, not what they want to do
- Acknowledges how difficult it is to walk through the door to see them
- Is conscious of your pain, your body language, your tone, your use of language
- Encourages cooperation
- Talks to you openly about money, about costs, and about cost-proportionality – there is no point in spending £2,500 arguing about £5,000 when there is only a 50 per cent chance of success
- Acknowledges that you are the boss, but knows that even so you can get it wrong
- Gives direction that you can follow
- Has counsellors, experts and a supportive team on hand
- Makes you feel personally comfortable and able to trust

- Is cautious and constructive, who listens and gives you the lead
- Is willing to give you clear direction as to a sensible way forward but, more important, will listen to you and act in accordance with your wishes
- Will be willing to try and stop you if you are trying to do a destructive act

An example of a destructive act would be insisting on naming third parties in adultery divorce proceedings. I refuse to do this, as there is no good purpose in involving a named third party in a family issue. Another example: insisting on following a course of action aimed at damaging the business or new relationship of your estranged partner. These are ultimately damaging for the whole family. Any good lawyer will always advise against following such a path.

Remember at all times: lawyers are not always right. They are not always the best judge of when proceedings should be issued. If you are vulnerable, it is too easy to be guided down a blind alley into injunction proceedings, issuing children proceedings or untimely divorce proceedings. Lawyers can guarantee very little in terms of outcome through a court, and do not have to live with the consequences of your actions. You are the one who will do that.

So you need to keep the lawyer in control, and you need to keep your mind focused on the impact of your actions in reality. This amounts to understanding and agreeing the risk implications of certain courses of conduct and being able to live with them. You do not want to provoke extreme reaction or take risks, particularly where children are involved. Work out what the scenarios could be if you do act in one way or another. And keep looking to alternative means of resolution.

If you do go and see your lawyer, remember a few important points at all times:

- It may be helpful to take a friend
- Going more slowly through the process often ends up leading to a quicker and more enduring outcome
- Just because you are feeling vulnerable, it does not mean you have to agree with the lawyer

How lawyers think

Lawyers like to be in control. They like their client to be in control, too, over the other party – proactive not reactive. They often want to work in a very structured and formalised way, and to do things in a certain order:

- Disclosure
- Questions
- Proposals

And they do all of this before exploring options together. This can have the effect of polarising decisions – painting people into a corner of expectation before addressing the family's needs. Once those positions are taken, it becomes more difficult to back away from them and seek resolution. Not impossible, just more difficult. But why add any extra difficulty to what is already a difficult situation?

Lawyers are wordsmiths. They generally use their letters to gain advantage should the matter come before the court, and to exert pressure on the other party to accede to their client's wishes. They can often use language that is completely unfamiliar to their client, and indeed their client's partner. That can lead to misunderstandings.

To be fair, I should point out that lawyers must be sure to protect themselves from accusations of negligence. It is for this reason that they are often defensive in their manner of communication with you. This approach can lead to lack of certainty on advice and a habit of setting out large parameters for potential settlement. They tend to use phrases such as:

- Quite likely
- Less than probable
- In the region of
- On the basis of your instructions
- Range of resolution
- Unpredictable nature of litigation

If you feel that terms like these are too vague to be helpful, don't hesitate to press your lawyer for something better. Remember: they are working for you. You're the boss.

Money money money

If you decide to choose the option of seeing matrimonial lawyers on financial issues arising out of divorce, and if you then decide ultimately to go to court rather than resolve matters, you often do that on the basis of the legal advice you receive. It is natural for lawyers to tell you what you want to hear. But what you want to hear is not always the same thing as what you should be hearing.

Here is an example of what I mean. After full disclosure of assets both sides agree that there is a financial pot of £500,000. The information that you have given to your matrimonial lawyer may lead them to say on your behalf that you could expect a reasonable settlement of the division of assets to give you half, i.e. £250,000. Your partner's lawyer may take the view that, from what they have told them, it is realistic for them to expect to receive more than half of the assets: £300,000. The other lawyer contends, on the basis of what their client has told them, that without £300,000 she could not adequately provide housing for the family.

So: the difference between the parties is £50,000. What happens next?

The two lawyers start exchanging letters. Counsel is brought in to advise as the litigation carries on and the case seems to be heading to a court hearing. After one year of proceeding to litigation, it is not at all difficult for the two lawyers, together with Counsel, to incur costs of £60,000. The financial difference that started the proceedings is smaller than the sums expended on fighting about it.

I often say that the combined costs of the matrimonial lawyers, when disputing financial issues, exceed or equal the sum that is in dispute. That can apply where the assets are relatively small, or when they're £1,000,000 or more.

If you want to avoid running up costs like that, it is vital to ensure that your solicitor is cost-proportionate – that you do not spend money without seeing a real potential financial benefit. They must also be flexible in their approach, and not rigidly stuck to a process that is designed for them and not for you. Otherwise they can send endless letters to each other about something relatively trivial.

Case example: Harry and Sally

Harry and Sally's daughter Edwina is desperate to join her friends on the school ski trip, which will cost £1200 (plus the equipment, clothing etc.). Harry is fixed that he will not pay more than £900 and Sally is insistent that on the maintenance she receives, she cannot afford to contribute anything towards the core cost of the trip. When Harry makes his proposal, to contribute £1000 at the most by way of compromise and not a penny more, he needs to be sure that he accepts that it's quite possible that Edwina will not be going on the school trip. That's the reality test. Can he live with the consequences, even if he thinks that Sally is being unreasonable?

Imagine the cost of lawyers dealing with this issue. Both Harry and Sally would end up paying more than the £200 difference between them.

Such discussions are not just expensive but largely fruitless. It is much easier just to agree to include all the various options that are proposed, and then you have the full information available to you, and that can be applied to the negotiations. When deciding on a path forward, it is easy to spend hundreds of pounds arguing about whether it is right or wrong, for example, to ask questions of an expert in this way or that way when you are jointly instructing them to prepare a report for you and your partner. It may be relevant to go down that path, but you need to be sure that you and your lawyer are doing so to reduce costs and not to incur more costs. Sometimes it is much easier just to agree to include all the various options that are proposed, and then you have all the information available to you and your partner, and they can all be applied to the negotiations. In addition, going through detailed expenditure in the bank accounts, asking for full details of cheques spent in the past, is not normally cost-proportionate. The cost of clarification can exceed the financial gain of having the value clarified. Choose your battles carefully, and do not get taken down blind alleys.

As in mediation and collaborative law, it is vital to have transparency on the financial disclosure before financial issues can be fully addressed. The solicitor will tend to work within their own comfort zone, doing things the way that works best for them. That is not the important point here. The important point is what will work best for you and your family.

Know your ABCs

Lawyers in negotiation, after getting comprehensive financial disclosure at the start, then negotiate from a high point and work down slowly. This is not necessarily the most cost-effective way to proceed. I use the alphabet as an analogy. If you are trying to get to the middle of the alphabet, M, why start at A when you could start at K? Each letter of the alphabet costs at least £25 in lawyers' fees. Why disrespect your partner and your partner's advisor in the hope of getting one over on them?

Communication – what's the best way?

A lawyer who is comfortable with letters and e-mails will try and channel all communication through the written word. The lawyer who is comfortable with telephone calls and round-table meetings, by contrast, will try and direct the negotiation to a table, rather as in collaborative law, but with the threat of litigation always in the background. Talking is often more cost-effective than exchanging letters.

Reassuringly expensive?

Some years ago an ad campaign for a brand of lager described it as 'reassuringly expensive.' Some people think the same way about lawyers, whatever the legal problem. And this may apply in matrimonial proceedings. We read in the newspapers that this or that celebrity or business tycoon has hired a lawyer charging top prices for their services in a divorce proceedings, and we think they're getting the best that money can buy.

I mean no disrespect to my high-paid colleagues, but more money does not necessarily buy better representation. I have been on the opposing side of lawyers from top London firms on numerous occasions. It is commonplace for their costs to be twice as high as my costs, or even higher, but their client is no more sad or content than my client when the case has finished.

Here is a typical scenario. I am approached by clients who

have been quoted £100,000 each on costs to see through a five-day hearing with a Queens Counsel in the Principal Registry dealing with the division of assets, and they have sought to come to mediation pending that final hearing. Even if one has numerous mediation appointments, ten or more, lasting two hours each, the overall cost of that would be £5,000 – 2.5 per cent of the potential costs of litigation from that point on. If the mediation is successful, so much the better! Not only do you avoid the costs of proceeding to trial, but also you own the outcome and the resolution that you have reached. You also do not run the risk that the litigation costs will be doubled because one of the parties decides to appeal. Why not protect the family wealth for the family? Why spend it on lawyers?

CHAPTER FOUR

Will I/Won't I?

If you have reached the conclusion that things cannot stay as they are, and that it is hard to envisage change, you need to prepare yourself for the consequences of splitting up.

There could be many reasons for thinking this way.

- Counselling is not working
- Counselling has been rejected
- One of you is having an affair
- You are in a trial period of separation
- All communication has ceased
- You simply see no alternative to separation

Whatever the reason, before you leave you need to identify where you stand. Once you make the leap it is sometimes difficult to stop your fall. You should be determined not to be impetuous, and to make sure you do not put in train a course of action that becomes irreversible. You need time and space to analyse the complexity of your situation, and to try and look at the position of the family objectively. You will want to understand your options. You will need to understand just how much control you will be able to exercise over the practicalities arising out of separation, and how much of the process is potentially out of your control.

Ultimately, you may want to know what the range of possible

outcomes could be, what they mean to you and your family, and what is the worst that could happen. This is the worst-case scenario, and you should always be aware of it and plan for it. And it can get even worse if you spend a lot of money in fighting it without success.

Your worst-case scenario will be particularly important in situations where litigation is more likely, such as:

- Your finances are complicated. For example, if you work together in a business, share the ownership of a business, or you have little knowledge or understanding of a business run by your partner, its value and earning potential.
- There is a fundamental lack of trust in your partner's ability to be honest about their financial position looking to the future. Your partner may be secretive about money – having a history of being less than candid with you and the authorities regarding his/her financial affairs. Full knowledge of the family's financial position and prospects is key to the making of any decisions regarding the future financial arrangements on separation.
- You or your partner have health problems, or suffer from depression which means that the decision-making could be flawed or badly motivated. Where this is the case, you will recognise that there is limited likelihood of being able to find a way forward by agreement. If one of you is disabled physically, then the whole question of your respective needs is going to have a bearing on the financial practicalities after separation.
- You believe that your partner will put their head in the sand and do all that they can to stand in the way of accepting the breakdown of the relationship, and to frustrate any change in circumstances, that too could be a real issue.

Getting a lawyer involved

If things are at an impasse for these or any other reasons, the time may have come to consult a lawyer – formally or informally. You don't necessarily need to be planning to take action or be seeking advice about whether to take action. In the beginning, consulting a lawyer may essentially be an opportunity for you to gather information. However, be careful, observant, and objective in your assessment of the lawyer and the approach they take.

It is essential to remember: once you instruct a lawyer, some of the control over the situation inevitably passes from you to them. Your lawyer will give you few categorical assurances about what your personal experience may be when you go down one route or another, and about what the outcome will be if the matter goes before the court. This is because few categorical assurances exist.

But they will also want you to choose them as your lawyer and so they are vulnerable to telling what you want to hear. This is especially likely when you go to a first brief appointment for no charge, where there's no commitment. It is tempting to think of the first free half hour as just free advice, but it is also the lawyer's opportunity for a sales pitch. I don't think that first appointments of less than an hour can give you any guidance in depth. That guidance should be followed up with a letter of advice. And it should be worth paying for. I have recently started doing this in my own practice because I am convinced that to have an impact, you need an hour at least and you need to value that time – as does the lawyer.

Your lawyer should encourage you to consider reconciliation, and talk about you working together with your partner. After taking on board you and your personal needs, he or she should be able to give you a lead that works for you, and is not stuck rigidly in a 'one size fits all' mentality.

Make sure, after your face-to-face appointment with the lawyer, that you have a clear picture of the limits of what the law can offer you, and think about what role you want the law to play in practical outcomes. Is the law to control you, or will you control the law and the lawyer?

You need to move on from such an appointment with a clear idea of the behaviour you expect of yourself. In all your dealings you have with your partner you should be determined to be:

- Constructive
- Trusting
- Positive
- Honest
- Respectful
- Forward-looking

Once your mind is made up and you know your marriage is over, now you have to decide how you are going to get through the process of dealing with the practicalities – and the emotional issues – that arise as your relationship implodes in front of your eyes. It is absolutely vital to remember one point:

Communication is everything

You must stay focused on the power of your communication and on every aspect of how your communication is received by your partner. When you are with them, your body language is vital. It takes deliberate effort to control it, and to be conscious of it at all times. It is simply no use to stonewall or behave towards your partner in a contemptuous way. You need to ensure that you appear receptive and open to what they wish to make clear to you. Ensure that the tone of your voice and the language you use are not harsh but gentle.

Similarly, it is unhelpful if you are critical in every

communication you have with your partner, or if every response you make to a criticism is defensive. You need to have a higher expectation of your own behaviour than of your partner's, and to try not to reflect negative behaviour from your partner back to them. Rise above it and set the example. The alternative is for your communication to spiral down and down to depths from which it will be hard to recover. For example, you don't need to respond to criticism of your extended family with criticism of your partner's. It is much more powerful to hold your counsel and to restrain your ability to hurt your partner's feelings and use loose words. Those words and thoughtless actions can always be brought back to you in future arguments, and when that happens, it will only have a negative impact.

It is vital to do all that you can to keep the channels of communication open. Above all, ensure that nothing you do can be interpreted as threatening, bullying, violent, physical or abusive. As soon as that happens, you find yourself in a position where your partner feels frightened, threatened, brow-beaten and vulnerable. Then there is no balance of power in the relationship. The whole balance is destroyed by the cloud of threat and fear hanging over one of the parties, and the response to that unacceptable behaviour is a rejection of all further communication through fear of your future reaction to your partner's rejection of your views. Any type of perceived threat is unacceptable behaviour when directed at a co-parent.

Communication is particularly important for your children's sake. They expect you, as their parents, to talk to each other, listen to each other, look to each other. And to be well behaved towards each other when you are in close proximity. Imagine, for example, at the time of collection or return from a contact visit, the example you give to your child if you do not look at your partner or talk to them, or if you refuse to listen to your partner but simply rush to distance yourself from them at the earliest opportunity. Again:

- Talk
- Listen
- Look
- Feel

You have the senses of sight, speech and hearing for a reason.

The pencil and the rubber band

Another cardinal rule:

Be flexible.

There is no point in being brittle. Brittle objects shatter when broken and cannot be put back together again. There is every benefit in being flexible to the point of being stretched in every direction. Many is the time that I have broken a pencil in front of a client and asked them to put the pencil back together again. When they fail to do it, I throw them a rubber band to stretch (as they're unable to break it) and then encourage them to put it round their wrist and keep it there. Then, whenever they feel that they are being emotionally stretched, they can stretch the rubber band as an example of holding things together and not irretrievably breaking points of contact.

I also emphasise certain points of behaviour. You will ride the storm better by ensuring you do not:

- Criticise
- Stonewall
- Ignore

- Treat with contempt

And be positive, too. Focus on parenting together when:

- Watching television
- Eating at meal times
- Coming face to face with your partner
- Going to parents' evenings at school

Go out of your way to compliment your partner. Support them. Make it clear to your children that you are working together as parents, and trying to avoid conflict and find a clear lead to give to them as parents.

In a new relationship? The children still come first

If you are in a new relationship, avoid worsening the situation by moving into it in an obvious manner. Emotions can become so heightened when that happens. Try and give your separation time and space without immediately cohabiting with your new partner. The new relationship can become a very real barrier, not only to rational communication with your former partner but also to a smooth transition for the children. They have to cope with two parents who cannot live together, but who are trying to work together for them as parents. Imagine being a child who feels deserted by one parent and who identifies with the parent with whom they live. The parent with whom they live also has a sense of betrayal. That child wants to be the centre of attention when contact is taking place. Instead of contact being all about them, the child, a new partner comes along as well. They perceive that their parent is looking after their new partner as much as them. They know they are no longer the centre of attention they crave to be.

Think about it.

First of all, handle this situation with your partner in a cooperative and constructive way. When the time comes to consider introducing your new partner to the children, stop and think. Discuss the situation with your former partner. Agree on how to break the news. Agree what to say, agree what the message is, then agree what the new partner's role is with the children. This is important to increase trust and reduce the feelings of threat that your former partner will experience when they think about your children meeting the person who has replaced them.

Remember, no one wants to be compared by their children with another parent. No one wants to have their sensitivity overlooked by their former partner and his or her new partner, particularly where there are children concerned.

It is important to make sure that the family stay on board too. Extended families always tend to have an opinion. The two parents can explain to their respective extended families how important it is for them all to be flexible, accepting and positive about changes that inevitably happen – such as new partners being introduced to the children

Things can be especially tricky if your partner has found someone new but you have not. You must try hard not to let your feelings of hurt and rejection make you obstruct your partner's wish to introduce their new partner to the children. You have to stifle your feelings and to find a way to make it possible. This may hurt in the short term. In the long term it will be better not just for your partner and your children but for you.

Vitally important: never underestimate the sense of rejection, especially if separation is swiftly followed by the introduction of your new partner to your children. The last thing you want is the fear of an unfavourable comparison by the children, when you have already been unfavourably compared to your partner's new partner by your former partner. You feel betrayed, and replaced as a spouse. And you fear you may go through the same experience as a parent. At this time there is also a risk that the children will be indulged and spoilt to encourage their acceptance of a new partner, and the children can take advantage of that. At the same time it may present the former partner with a real dilemma of not being able to afford to give the children the same indulgence.

All this is very difficult for whichever partner has a new relationship. They want to show off their children to the new partner, quite understandably. Perhaps less understandably, they might want to show off the new partner to their children. However proud they may be of their new relationship, the timing of the communication and the ability of the child and the former partner to adjust must be taken into account.

If you do have a new relationship, ensure that your children and your grieving partner see it as being given second priority. They have the greatest need of your focus at this difficult time, whatever your personal needs might be. Focus on making a plan to give the children time, time with you on their own. Separate this from time with your new partner on your own. Consider what you can say to the children together with your existing partner, and whether it is an appropriate time to talk to the children. Also consider whether each of the children needs one-on-one time with you, and indeed with your partner.

Be circumspect in what you say to friends, because what you say may well be repeated back to your partner with an unintended twist. This often arises out of a misunderstanding. That can create further risk in the channel of direct communication between you and your partner, and you and your partner's parenting relationship with the children.

The children: preparation for the pain

Be very clear about one thing: children suffer when their parents go through divorce. But the suffering can be minimised if you think clearly about their needs and work together as parents to meet them. Above all, conflict between their parents is a very clear sign that that child will have a hard time adjusting to the demands of the world. It is what professionals call a bad indicator. The good indicators are (A) a clear lead from the parents with whom they share time and (B) financial stability.

If possible, talk with the children together with your existing partner before any physical separation, and explain to them what is happening in their life. It really helps the children to have a clear lead from both parties without conflict being shown as to what they will be doing together for them as the children's parents.

The core message to the children is that it is not their fault that their mother and father cannot live together. Reasons do not have to be given. They need to know that both their parents work together for them, and that both their parents continue to love them. They have no wish to hear their parents criticise each other, and they do not want or need to be asked to parent a vulnerable parent when they are but a child. Different children have different needs, depending on their age, their sex, their attachments.

As babies, children need to:

- Bond with both parents
- Have regular contact with both parents
- Feel secure

As toddlers, children need to have:

- Regular physical affection
- Regular reassurance from both parents
- Predictable treatment

As nursery school children, children need:

- Predictable routines
- Feeling positive about both parents

As junior-school children, they need:

- To build their self-esteem
- To feel good about themselves

As pre-teens they need:

- The chance to explore their strong sense of right and wrong
- To be relieved of the burdens of adulthood

As teens they need:

- Freedom to explore
- Friendship and social life
- To be consulted on things that affect them

Children do not need to shoulder adult responsibilities and to be called on to be their parent's carer. Children do need to understand that divorce is a grownup problem, and one over which they have no control. They need the opportunity to express their feelings, and they need to feel they have a voice – that they are listened to.

Too often children are kept in the dark by their parents when the parents know they are separating. For some reason the parents believe that they can keep their difficulties hidden from the children, but the children always seem to know so much more than the parents give them credit for.

Trying to keep secrets is a terrible and potentially destructive mistake. There is nothing more fertile than a child's imagination, and to leave a child guessing rather than knowing, and without a clear lead and explanation from both their parents, is a dangerous thing to do.

Certainty of unconditional love is essential for helping

children through their parents' divorce. The children need not just the ability to love and feel positive about both their parents, but the feeling that both their parents love them and will continue to work together for them in a continuing long-term relationship. Frequently children will feel that they have contributed to the reasons for their parents' separation, and they need to be told quite clearly that this is not the case. Try to do everything you can to ensure that they do not blame themselves for your problems.

Your children also need you to be honest with them, without being critical of their other parent, and to be reassured about their future and the fact that they will have a continued relationship with you both, even if it is that you can no longer live together.

Just imagine the joy of a child seeing their biological parents working together for them and not in conflict over them. The child's confidence and capacity to adapt grow massively. Parents' Evenings are no longer a threat. Collection and return from contact visits are no longer a point of pressure. Mixed messages that the child has to try and interpret come to an end. Children find it harder to play one parent off against the other. All this sets your child up for a great future in the life that awaits them in the outside world.

It is worth emphasising again that you must never criticise your co-parent to your children. On the contrary, compliment them. Again: no child wants to hear one parent criticised or attacked by the other parent, Their body and mind are part and parcel of both parents, and both parents are their role models on life. Think about it. Put yourself in their position. Would you have liked it if one of your parents had complained to you about the other?

CHECKLIST: Talking to children

- It is good to talk to them together
- Talk to the children even if you can only say you are talking together as parents

- It is OK to say 'Mummy and Daddy cannot live together, but will always love you and work together for you as your parents' – if that is your plan, which it ought to be
- Talk to the children to inform them so that they know what is happening. Then they do not have to fantasise as to what might be happening
- Talk to the children so that they know you are working together for them as parents
- Agree your script with your partner and stick to it
- You do not have to tell the children you have got it all sorted, just that you are trying
- It is a great motivation to you as parents to keep trying and make it happen
- When you have a plan, tell the children together what that plan is
- Parental guidance by both parents without conflict is just what the children want

Get a financial framework

The financial pressures, if you are preparing to split up or have just split up, are immense. Your standard of life on separation is likely to drop by 30 per cent, and that is a fact of life that comes with separation. You and your partner will both have to make adjustments. Money will play an increasingly important part in your planning.

One thing is vital: you need to have a clear budget, even if it does not come naturally to you. You must work out your regular financial needs, and assess your regular dependable income. You need to ensure that your budget is within your income, so that your debts do not increase. Your plan should be to reduce debts, not to increase them.

There is often a tendency to splash out financially when you separate. This may be because you are angry and believe you deserve money to replace your departed partner. It may be because you want to punish your partner. You may not see why you and the children should be worse off.

The absent partner may feel guilty and therefore prepared to do anything financially to reduce the amount of criticism levelled at them in the hope of maintaining a good link with the children, who are open to your influence as they live with you. This only creates greater problems for the future.

Consider breaking down your budget into the following areas:

- Property costs
- Financial costs
- Personal living costs
- Car costs
- Leisure costs
- Costs per child

Some points to pay attention to

Look at your mortgage and your mortgage options. If you are going to be spending money on two homes, not one, is it possible in the short term to reduce the monthly mortgage payments to interest-only payments, or to extend the term for repayment, or indeed obtain a mortgage holiday, without incurring a penalty from the bank?

Look at your credit cards and try and stop using them. Turn your attention to your debit card linked into your current account. Consider simply making repayments on the credit cards. Close down or freeze cards where you both have access but which is the responsibility of just one of you. You need to be in control of expenditure. You need to balance outgoings against income. The one thing you do not need is greater indebtedness that reduces the options, in housing especially, for the future. Good housing options are vitally important.

If you have a joint account, make sure that the overdraft limit is clearly specified, and that you work within your current funds. If you are unable to do so, then separate the standing orders and the joint account into two individual accounts, and agree budgets that can work for you both in the short term.

With regard to your household bills, find out whose name they are in. If you are no longer living in the house and your partner is expected to meet the expense of the household bill, then put those household bills into your partner's name and get them to sign the relevant forms. In general: take control of the expenditure, talk about the finances, write down your income, write down your needs, and keep a regular eye on ensuring that you both do not exceed your expenditure targets or your combined income.

Don't be extravagant. Be sure not to go buying expensive cars or capital items. Do not take expensive holidays. Do not take out loans in your own name to fund what you cannot afford. You will only be storing up problems for the future.

Look at your prospective income, and not just from employment. What are the benefits and tax credits that may be available to you or your partner, such as Child Tax Credit, Working Tax Credit and Child Benefit? Your eligibility to these changes on separation. Look at the opportunities to increase your pay, and look at the opportunities of the family to increase the family income as a whole. Consider Housing Benefit and the availability of Council Tax rebates.

Understand the capital assets and liabilities. Draw together a Schedule of Assets detailing the value of the following:

- Assets in joint names
- Assets in your name

- Assets in your partner's name
- Any particular issues that you think need to be clarified regarding the assets

It is OK for short-term financial arrangements to be different from long-term financial plans. The short-term needs will almost always be different from long-term needs. Your finances change, but it will take time to change them – and that is a long-term plan. In the short term, you have to pay the full mortgage and any interest on loans and credit cards in order to hold things together. This will make them easier to regularise.

If you overspend in the short term, you can reduce your options in the long term. That's why I advise financial caution, even if it is painful, at the time of separation.

Note: financial matters are discussed in much greater detail in the 'Money Matters' chapter.

Look out for everyone's well-being

Important as it is to be cautious and careful about financial issues, do not overlook the need to care for each member of your family – and that includes yourself. Find the financial balance that works adequately for you all. Also, it is important to remember that financial stability and security help provide emotional well-being for a child, and your children should be protected from the financial anxieties of their parents. Do not over-involve a child in these adult issues. Simply explain that you, as the child's parents, are making a plan.

It is also important to take care of yourself emotionally and encourage your partner to do the same. You both need time for yourself. You need the opportunity to talk about your dilemmas. That may be in the form of counselling. It may be through friends – but as supporters, not as advisors! It may simply be by having the opportunity to have time on your own without having pressure put upon you or being made to feel guilty. You can help each other to find this time.

Try not to plan your talking time when delivering or collecting the children on contact visits. Arrange a time each week or month, away from contact visits – a telephone call, a cup of coffee, a parent planning meeting focused on the children. What are they up to? What are the issues? How can you help each other parent together and give a clear lead to your children? Not least, this has enormous benefits for the children because they see their parents working together for them.

You also need to consider your physical health. What exercise have you normally taken? What exercise should you start to take? The release of exercise will help you think clearly. Look after your body, thereby giving your brain space and peace.

Timing is important

Do not put yourself in the position of riding the storm of separation, and making practical arrangements, if it is obviously the wrong time. The period of separation is turbulent whatever the circumstances. It is so difficult if other problems come along at the same time. If somebody in the family has been seriously ill, or if there has been a death of a close family member, it cannot be a good time to address problems in your relationship and to separate. Consider the timing of the school year; exams that the children are doing; and when family, friends or other support may be most available to your partner.

When dealing with the problems of a broken relationship, the prospects of a successful resolution are inevitably heightened by finding the right time to deal with the right problem in the right way – and preferably with assistance from the right person and with your partner in the right frame of mind.

So if your wife's father has just died or is dying, stop and think. If your husband has just lost his mother, stop and think. If one of you has lost their employment, or is experiencing health problems, stop and think. Consider the enormous impact of what you are about to do, and consider how best to proceed. Test the reality of the situation as it will be as the weeks and months go by, if you choose to act now rather than wait for a better time.

Remember: you married for a good reason. You chose a good time to marry. You planned to do it. You made sure it was a time when you could all be at your best for the event. Well, the same applies for divorce. You can get divorced right now. But will there be a better time when could you get divorced?

CHAPTER FIVE

How To Work Through It

Once the decision to separate has been made, and you have done your research as to which process you believe will best suit you and your partner and your family as a whole, it's time to look at the practicalities. It is all very well knowing the theory and wanting to find a consensual way forward, but putting it into practice can be difficult.

In the same way that it is often said there are many different ways of skinning a rabbit, there are many different ways of dealing with the practicalities arising out of separation. They all have their own advantages and disadvantages, but those advantages and disadvantages need to be measured against:

- The time it takes to find a solution
- The emotional tensions in getting to resolution
- The cost of the process
- The quality of the outcome

At one end of the spectrum are the people who decide to do nothing. They do not wish to be active through the process, they just let it happen and see how things pan out. That is a fairly extreme lack of reaction to a very real problem.

At the other end of the spectrum, some people think that they will never find their own solution, and that for some reason judges in courtrooms are best placed to tell them what the best outcome for their problem is. That is a similarly extreme abrogation of responsibility, and an over-reaction to an intractable problem. Sometimes it is inevitable for psychological or physical health reasons, cultural differences, or for reasons tied into the complexity of the finances, or where it is impossible for the two parties to engage in rational negotiation and discussion even with assistance and advice. But unless it really is completely unavoidable for one of these reasons, you should regard going to court as a very last resort.

I think that the quality of the outcome will largely be determined by two equally important things:

- The amount of direct communication that goes on between you and your partner through the process of parting
- The amount of communication that goes on after the solution has been reached

Another way of looking at it is: how will your children look back over their lifetime at the resolution reached by their parents? Was it an example to them of how to behave, or was it an example of how not to behave? How were they affected by their parents' behaviour through separation? You should try to keep this question in your mind throughout the divorce process.

Resolution, resolution, resolution

When deciding on process, resolution is the word to have at the top of your mind. Resolution is the key, and the will, energy and commitment to resolution mean everything; but it takes two to tango. There is no right process. The right process is the process that reaches resolution, ideally consensual resolution in which each party is equally unhappy about or accepting of the way the future looks. Once resolution has been reached, there is little point in looking back. The only purpose becomes using the resolution as a springboard for the changed family dynamic of the future.

The five different processes available to the couple, if counselling is not the answer, are:

Mediation

Sometimes with the help of a local priest or vicar, or a family member, but more often with the help of a trained Family Mediator. Mediators are impartial. They encourage contributions by both sides and a balance of power between the two sides. Sometimes mediators co-mediate, and the way they work can be an example to you and your partner of how future communication could work.

Collaboration

These are round-table meetings always with both parties and their lawyers present. The lawyers can give advice within the meeting to help you find a resolution.

Negotiation

This can take place at a round table or through correspondence or against the timetable of court proceedings.

Arbitration

This is similar to litigation insofar as you are giving responsibility to the arbitrator to find the best outcome for your problem, rather than taking responsibility for finding that outcome for yourself.

Litigation: the last (and worst) option

Too often the soft option is to leave open the threat of litigation, or to issue proceedings supposedly as 'a non-aggressive act' in order to set a timetable to finality. It is a dangerous road to travel. To issue proceedings on children or financial matters is to give up control and let go of the channels of direct communication between you and your partner. It amounts to placing your trust in your lawyer's powers of argument in order to achieve the best statistical outcome. But it disregards the long-term consequences of giving away your control over your separation. Think long and hard before issuing proceedings.

On the other hand, entering into an agreement where you reject litigation, or the threat of litigation, and seek to find your own solutions to your own problems, can leave the process open to abuse. This is particularly true where there is an imbalance of power that is not controlled – for example, if one person takes an intractable approach and is simply trying to force their preconceived solutions on the process. Often one partner has more information, and greater knowledge and control over the finances than the other. That power imbalance needs to be remedied.

Whichever route you go down, the skill level of the mediator, collaborative lawyer or solicitor cannot be assumed. And it is of vital importance. They are not all good. Some just don't get it. In the case of collaborative law, the skill levels of both solicitors and their commitment to the process is of particular and fundamental importance.

This is not an issue that can be dealt with by processes. It has to be dealt with by skilled individuals.

The options in detail

Doing nothing

Doing nothing is a real option. For many couples it is an option that they take for months or years, but more often than not the period of doing nothing eventually comes to an end.

Doing nothing amounts to allowing the status quo to stand and being purely reactive. It is a way of dealing with issues, avoiding conflict, avoiding finality, and coexisting after the relationship has broken down. This option should never be ignored and should always be considered, so that if you do decide to do something, it is a positive act taken deliberately and with purpose.

Doing nothing is by no means a perfect option. It means leaving the outcome uncertain. You do not know if and when there may be divorce proceedings, or a dispute over the children or financial proceedings in the future. Doing nothing also has an impact on your children: they do not know with clarity the nature of their parents' relationship. On the positive side, the acute stress, strain and grieving process for the couple and the family – all of which come with divorce – can be avoided. But remember that other strains take their place.

Also sometimes it makes no sense financially to crystallize a position – for example, when a personal economic problem or a national economic downturn is affecting family finances. Alternatively, there may be strong reasons related to health or children's wellbeing and education that make it sensible to do nothing. An example would be if your children were in the final months of important exams, or if one partner's mother or father were in critically poor health.

If you are thinking about doing nothing, consider asking a lawyer to give you two hours of fixed-fee advice to help you process financial discussions. Or meet with a Financial Advisor to help you understand the figures, options and reality of different scenarios if you were to stop doing nothing.

Mediation

It is no coincidence that the government is pushing for a change in the mind-set of separating couples from taking proceedings to going to mediation. Twenty years ago few people knew what the word 'mediation' meant. Now there is a much more general understanding of its meaning and purpose.

Mediation has long been at the forefront of resolution of conflict. Its purpose is to have a trained professional help people in conflict find their own solutions to their own problems. Surely that is what we should all do – find our own solutions to our own problems – because there is no 'one size fits all' solution.

Family mediators are trained specialists who try to help separating couples find their own solutions. They use a range of skills to ensure that couples who voluntarily enter into the process have a balance of power in discussing and understanding the options and pathways available to them. This is aimed at enabling them to choose from those options for their own family futures. You need to understand how mediation works, how it gets started, and how it proceeds.

The principles of mediation:

- It is voluntary
- The mediators are impartial
- The process is confidential
- There are no secrets
- The clients make the decisions
- Mediators do not advise one or another party but give both parties the same information at the same time

Mediation usually lasts for between 2 and 5 sessions of about 90 minutes each.

I may be biased because I do mediation myself, but I think

this is the best option. Mediators normally know the law. They know how to read the signs. They have had good training on how to listen, how to listen to tone, and how to look at body language. They have good language skills and reframe potentially negative comments into a positive communication. They keep couples heavily focused on the way forward and on the needs of the children in a positive and constructive way, looking at the family's needs as a whole. Because they know how to listen, they can use words precisely and assist each of you to have a better ability to listen to each other, as opposed to what you think they are saying. They also have a great capacity to normalise problems that are obviously barriers in your approach to working together into the future.

Mediators have clear ground rules that they insist on setting out before the mediation process can begin. In addition to explaining that they are impartial and will not give advice, they emphasise certain points:

- Everything is meant to be confidential
- The proceedings are 'without prejudice', meaning not to be repeated in court but said in this safe environment where people speak freely in the hope of progress and moving on, so that is the focus and no one is being defensive as they would in an adversarial environment
- What is said cannot later be used in court (although this cannot be absolutely guaranteed in some proceedings where children are involved)

Confidentiality is not relevant to financial disclosure. If you have just won £1,000,000 on the lottery, you have to reveal it. At all times those in the mediation process must be honest about their financial circumstances.

The mediator also will breach the confidentiality if there is a risk of significant harm to any individual.

The mediator is trained to ensure that there is a balance of power within the mediation process between both participating parties. And full cooperation is essential. Mediation cannot work if it is forced on parties and not entered into voluntarily.

Outside experts

Even though the family mediator leads the way, other experts can be used in the mediation process. They should be impartial and should be instructed by both partners. Indeed, there is no reason why legal advisors should not be involved in the mediation process. Mediators always advise clients to take legal advice in any event. It is important for both clients to know that they have access to legal and other advice throughout the process, even if those advisors do not join them in the mediation sessions themselves. But there is no reason why they should not, if that is what the clients want and the mediator agrees.

Outside experts can be called on to give their view on, for example, the value of a business, the value of a pension, or the value of properties. Or they can give general financial advice. They might be child psychologists, barristers, or solicitors. But whomever you turn to, you need to ensure that their involvement is cost-proportionate. Make sure you're deriving sufficient benefit to justify that extra expense.

While mediators will always encourage the participants to take legal advice, this is particularly true where joint proposals have been reached as to the way forward in either the short term or the long term. The solution will have been reality-tested in mediation to assess the position each party would be placed in – which is the whole point of using a mediator. The idea is to empower you both to tell your lawyers what you want and why as a result of a lot of discussion in mediation.

Those joint proposals are not legally binding. Before they are turned into a legally binding arrangement, if that is what you want, it is prudent to get advice on whether the solution you've found can work within a legal framework. This means that you can explain to the lawyer why you do not want him or her to unstitch the detailed proposals you have reached. And make no mistake: some lawyers try to get outcomes that fit in with their preconceived notions of what the proper outcome should be, instead of the outcome you want. The advisors can then turn the proposals into a binding document, if that is what you want.

Mediators would say that their process is quicker, cheaper and leads to better outcomes because they are your outcomes and not your lawyers' outcomes.

How it happens

Before you are accepted into the mediation process, it is important to have a Mediation Information and Assessment Meeting (MIAM) with a mediator in order to establish if your situation is appropriate for mediation. (There is more about MIAMs in the chapter 'Children: Do They Have a Voice?') This will also help you to better understand the process and also understand the alternative processes that are available to you.

In the great majority of cases, the format of mediation involves both parties sitting in a room together with one mediator and addressing issues directly to each other. But there can be two co-mediators and this may be a good thing in certain situations:

- Where there is a high level of anxiety about mediation
- Where a gender balance of a male and female mediator would help
- Where the legal knowledge of a mediator would help

- Where a psychological background would help deal with power balance issues between the clients
- Where there are children issues (not always a natural strength of lawyers)

Lawyer-mediators learn an immense amount about people and family dynamics by co-mediating with mediators from a psychological background. I count myself as one of that fortunate band of mediators with a legal background.

It is possible for mediation to take place from separate rooms (this is called 'shuttle mediation'), but mediators will always strive to ensure that both parties get into the same room so that they can communicate their views directly to each other and listen to each other.

Mediation can be helpful whatever your circumstances – whether you are living together, or living separately; whether you are married or unmarried; whether you have already dealt with the issues beforehand and wish to review them; or indeed if you are already divorced.

With regard to financial issues, it is not possible to have those discussions within the mediation process unless you are both transparent in your financial declarations. In most instances you will be required to give full and open disclosure of your precise financial position. If you wish to incorporate an agreement within an order of the court by agreement, the court could overturn any agreement where incomplete information had formed the basis of the decision-making. If you misrepresent your finances in your financial disclosure, the court has the power to overturn any consent order you obtain, and to start the whole process over again on the basis of the greater financial information now available.

Why choose mediation? My three main arguments in favour:

- You keep control of your own situation

- Conflict is reduced
- You can focus in your own way on the issues that you each wish to resolve

Collaboration

There is as much confusion over the meaning of collaboration and collaborative law now as there was in the 1990s over the meaning of the word mediation.

Collaboration involves working with a collaborative family lawyer. Four people sit around a table – the couple and their respective solicitors. They sign a Participation Agreement indicating that they will find a solution without recourse to the courts to litigate their divorce, or the financial issues, or children issues arising out of separation. The only use of the court will be to obtain Consent Orders.

And then they work hard, sometimes with advice present in the room, to find solutions that work for their particular circumstances. Again, outside experts are frequently drawn into the process: life coaches, counsellors, psychotherapists, psychologists, financial advisors, actuaries, pension advisors, accountants, surveyors. These experts are sensitive to the commitment that the couple have made to find the best solution by agreement rather than through conflict. You can bring in whoever is needed to help provide information that will help you find agreement with the benefit of your legal advice.

The collaborative process is a new approach, changing the way people think about family law while also involving legal advice. It is for couples who genuinely seek a fair solution and want to minimise the pain of family breakdown but need advice about how to do that. It is for couples who feel the need to have a lawyer with them at all times in negotiations and discussions. This is more often the case where one party has much more financial knowledge than the other, and where both parties and their lawyers are determined not to abuse the process of collaboration but to reach agreement for the good of the family as a whole.

Collaboration's unique advantage for the right couples and the right lawyers lies in the signed agreement not to go to court. Not only do all four parties sign an agreement that they will not litigate, but they also make it clear that they will not threaten to litigate the other. Instead they will seek to find joint decisions about financial and child care arrangements, focused on the needs of the family as a whole.

The process of collaborative law should reduce the amount of inter-solicitor correspondence to a minimum. Collaboration is all about both parties being sat round a table with each of their respective solicitors in the same room, face-to-face. The couple deal with the matter direct and not through the solicitors.

However, for collaboration to work both parties need to have a genuine desire to really find a sound, practical solution. If the process breaks down, the collaborative lawyers will withdraw from the process. Then the couple will need to find other solicitors with the inevitable duplication of costs.

Both parties, as in mediation, need to be completely transparent about their finances. And both parties need to be absolutely focused on reaching a solution without going to court.

The comfort factor of having your own solicitor alongside you and involved in the discussions can be extremely helpful. They will help you set the agenda and set the pace. They will try and be creative in the options available to you, and will be open about the advice they are giving you within the room, so that there is no hidden agenda.

The collaborative lawyer's advice should not be about getting the best outcome for their client but about getting the best outcome for the family as a whole while also listening to the needs of the couple. So it is important that there is a high level of trust between all four participants.

Collaboration is a great idea, but very dependent on a lot of good will. The collaboratively trained lawyers must have a real determination to hold back on partiality and not to be overly motivated by the desire to obtain the best outcome for their client. They should be focused on looking for the best outcome for the family as a whole. The couple must also be prepared for possible problems. You cannot always choose your partner's lawyer, and that lawyer will not always be a collaborative lawyer. Also, it is difficult to commit to the Participation Agreement blindly. You end up relying on your lawyer's interpretation and advice. He or she may say that your case is suitable for collaboration and that they can work with the other lawyer in the collaborative process. But because you have not been here before, you are dependent on the judgement of someone you haven't known for very long. By the same token, if they advise against it, you may think it's appropriate nonetheless. What do they know?

In my view, collaboration is a bit of a compromise between mediation and negotiation. Although collaborative lawyers are meant to train in mediation techniques, they often lean more comfortably towards the negotiation style that they have been trained to have as lawyers. The boundaries of discussion can be grey and confusing.

Negotiation through solicitors

Negotiation, like collaboration, can take place around a table with solicitors present. But in most ways the two approaches are radically different. For one thing, no Participation Agreement has been signed. This means that those solicitors can continue to act for both parties if consent is not reached and the matter be taken to court. Negotiations close no options, including whether to pursue mediation, collaboration or litigation in the future. It can often be more hard-headed and positional than collaboration and mediation, but not necessarily so.

Negotiation in a single room is relatively rare, however. Rather than round-table meetings, it more often takes the form of exchanges of correspondence between lawyers – and posturing. One trouble with this form of communication is that the lawyers' words often do not reflect the precision of the client's instructions, and can be formulated in a way that increases the tensions between the parties – rather like Chinese whispers.

The correspondence process is also very costly. Imagine that A wants to ask B a question in an attempt to reach a resolution. A contacts her solicitor, her solicitor contacts B's solicitor, and he contacts B, his client. B replies to his solicitor, who then replies to A's solicitor, who then relays the response to A's original question. That is six different sequences of communication – all capable of misinterpretation – and of being charged! At £25 per communication, plus VAT, that's a combined bill of £180. A request by a solicitor to a solicitor – 'please can I have the table tennis table for the children' – could cost more than the table.

How negotiators work

More often than not, negotiation through solicitors takes place against the background of a threat of litigation. Solicitor listens to client and establishes the facts from his or her perspective, and then seeks to get the best outcome. That is to say, the best outcome for their client.

Family solicitors are skilled negotiators, assertive and often directive about the way they think is the right way to achieve the best outcome. They are encouraged to deal with matters in a non-confrontational way and avoid inflammatory letters, and are required to retain professional objectivity and put the interests of the children first.

But often they can find themselves being encouraged by their client to take an aggressive, dogmatic stance in negotiation, and they are reluctant to counter their paying client's instructions. Solicitors have costs targets to reach and need work to do if they're to reach them. It is easier to hit your budget with this type of client. A client who pursues every detail aggressively and asks the solicitor to write letters about every point arising in negotiation can easily be worth four times as much as a client who seeks resolution as speedily and painlessly as possible. Even if you can afford to waste all that money, and even if you feel genuinely and unfairly aggrieved, resist the impulse to go down this route. The only person who benefits from it is your lawyer.

Again, you must remember that commercial considerations abound in law firms. Firms have different areas of work that they do, all of them with varying levels of profitability. Is it any wonder that some large firms have a reputation for overlooking the opportunity to compromise while seeking to get the best outcome for their client – even if the cost is exorbitant?

A good example of this is joint instruction, where a single surveyor is instructed to value a couple's jointly held properties. The sensible, cost-effective way of doing this is to include all possible considerations that might affect the valuation – potential planning permission, tenants, the road that may (or may not) be coming through. The surveyor can do his or her work and get back with a comprehensive estimate of value which puts everything into a single document. But sometimes one side, all too often under the guidance of the solicitor, tries to define the terms of the valuation. X should not be put in, Y must be put in, Z can only be put in on this or that condition. While trying to resolve these trivial and simply unnecessary 'issues', the two sides can exchange ten letters. That posturing can cost the separating couple £250-500 between them.

Work together, not separately

Solicitors will often seek to obtain a margin of financial advantage by obtaining their own expert evidence about value of properties, accountant's advice and financial advice before agreeing to jointly instruct an expert if the values that they have identified cannot be agreed. This can ratchet up costs, and heighten tensions and emotions, and worsen the breakdown of the relationship between the couple. For example, how normal is it for a person to want to ask his own accountant for a valuation of the business he runs rather than an independent, unknown accountant who will not continue to work for him in the future?

Or: if you, as one of the parties, want to stay in the family home and buy out your partner's interests, how normal is it for you to try and find a valuer who will attribute a lower value to the home than you believe it is worth, while your partner tries to find a valuer who will attribute a higher value? Why not just trust in the gods and get a joint surveyor? You have to work out what you are doing and why, and that's fine. Just don't kid yourself about what you are doing. And if you want to play games, be prepared to pay for it.

However, two skilled negotiating solicitors are frequently capable of assisting and advising a matter to resolution, without excluding their option of litigating if that is not possible. They can do this in a prompt, effective and cost-effective manner, reflecting the wishes of both their clients. Two solicitors provide early financial disclosure and identify the size of the matrimonial pot which includes capital, pensions and income. They listen to their clients, advise as to the options that are in the zone and realistic. In meetings they explore their options and the best way forward for the family as a whole without being focused on getting 'the best financial deal for my client.' They take account of the big picture.

Sadly, this kind of cooperation is relatively rare. Most lawyers – and their clients – think the lawyer's role is to get the best outcome for the individual regardless of family dynamics. It's a short-term fix!

You need to make sure that the work that they are doing for you is to your benefit and your family's benefit, and cost-proportionate. You need to understand the costs implications at all times and be conscious that you have control of how the matters have been dealt with by the solicitor acting for you.

Arguments for negotiation

Often negotiation through solicitors is an appropriate way to proceed, particularly where there are power imbalances, or where there is a lack of transparency on finances. It can be important when the two parties are at different places emotionally and where there is a need to seek a resolution that is not at the right time for both parties, and when there is a problem that needs to be resolved regardless.

Solicitors can encourage you, the client, not to do nothing and not to frustrate working towards resolution by pressing the pace of resolution regardless of whether both parties consider it to be at the right time between the right persons dealing with a common problem.

Another reason to use a solicitor in these circumstances is that the greater the asset, the greater the risk when it comes to negotiating resolution without hands-on legal advice.

Naturally, people going through divorce often do not feel confident in their ability to deal with an alien subject. Fear of the unknown can be a strong motivator behind the decision to instruct a solicitor to negotiate on your behalf against the threat of litigation, and this is because of lack of confidence in your own capacity to control more direct negotiations with your partner.

How much easier it is for us to rely on the lawyer to get the best outcome for us and tell us that it is fair.

All the above approaches are so much better than going to court. Court is costly, out of your control, a poor method for dealing with future problems, and an abrogation of responsibility.

However, solicitors are not always the best at empowering their clients to find their own solutions and to enable the clients to take responsibility for their own solutions.

Litigation

Once you issue proceedings you really are making it clear that you are handing over the decision-making to another. You are accepting that you cannot be sure of the outcome, as courts have a wide discretion, and you are damaging the prospect of direct communication with your partner to find an agreed solution between you. You are looking for a judgement, rather than resolution.

Picture the final scenario at court. You are in one room with your solicitor and your barrister. Your partner is in another room with their solicitor and their barrister. The barristers have a corridor near a coffee machine where they discuss your case away from you and your solicitor in an attempt to achieve the end you seek, or the end that they seek for you which can be very different.

You do not know what is said in that meeting; nor do you know how things are said in that meeting. In addition, you do not know how what is said is reported back to your partner. Neither you nor your partner have the chance to ask questions to each other face-to-face, and to interpret the answer, or take account of the manner in which the answer is given by the tone or body language of your partner.

Sometimes litigation is inevitable where the assets are

complex, where there is lack of transparency, where there are health issues, or where one party is not ready or able to engage. But sometimes it is highly avoidable through plain speaking face-to-face with or without advice.

To put any litigation into perspective, think about the advice your lawyer is giving you as to outcome. Is it based on information that they have gained from you? Is it based on information they have gained from your partner and/or his solicitor? Is the advice objective, or is it subjective? If they assure you that you will get a certain outcome, ask them to write to you and guarantee that outcome.

But it is highly unlikely that any lawyer will do that. This is because they do not know categorically what a judge will order.

Ask them about timescales. Whereas the mediative and the collaborative, and indeed the negotiation through solicitor process, can all be effective quite swiftly after financial disclosure, the litigation process is – and is likely to continue to be – protracted and subject to delay. It is quite realistic to wait 6 months to achieve a negotiated settlement at court with a judge's help, or 12 months for a judge's pronouncement about financial proceedings from the original issue of proceedings.

The court's options are limited compared to what can be agreed, and often by not talking and trying to reach agreement you cut off your nose financially to spite your face. Instead of a process that can treat you as two individuals seeking a flexible outcome, a court process has to fit you into their mould.

Think how painful it must be to sit through three days of a hearing you do not really understand, with many of the issues you want discussed ignored or overlooked, with barristers using age-old tactics to discredit each of you in the eyes of the court, and to exaggerate one position over the other. They are not frightened by arguing, or by a contest. That is why they are family barristers. That is one reason why they chose the job.

During that time where you give away control of your own financial destiny to your lawyer, the breakdown of the relationship can be so deep that it is difficult to build back any channel of communication. It is unlikely that you will find that you or your partner will consider each other's advocate non-adversarial within a court process.

Litigation is about the individuals and not the family. It is about outcome and not relationships. It should be used only in the most extreme circumstances.

CHAPTER SIX

Children: Do They Have a Voice?

There are a number of technical legal issues you have to deal with when you and your divorcing partner have children together. But none of them is as important as the golden rule which I have already mentioned several times in this book:

Avoid hostility

Implacable hostility to your partner is something you must try to avoid at all costs. Needless to say, it is bad – no, terrible – for your children. But it is also against your own interests. If the court interprets your behaviour as a parent as being hostile without good reason, they are very able to reverse decisions that have been made either by the court itself or by you both as parents. They will not countenance it.

Case example: an extreme

After numerous court cases, Jonny, the only son of Dick and Emma, is ordered to live with his mother and have alternate weekend contact with Dick. This contact never seems to work out. Emma never approves of it and frustrates it at every opportunity. The opportunity to frustrate arises when Jonny is ill or has other arrangements at the weekend such as birthday parties or sporting events. Now, longing for a quiet life, Jonny has taken to agreeing with Emma when she says, 'Oh you don't want to see Dad this weekend, do you?' The result is that in spite of Dick's four applications to the court over the past 30 months asking for Jonny's contact with him to be upheld, which it has been on every occasion, Emma continues to frustrate. This time, Dick applies for Jonny's residence to move to him and reassures the court that he will ensure that Jonny has whatever contact the court orders with Emma. The judge has had enough over the last three years and makes the order that Dick seeks. Jonny moves in with his father.

If the parents are so hostile that they cannot make reasoned decisions, then on occasion a Guardian is appointed to represent the best interests of the child. If you are getting to the stage of considering using the court as the forum to make decisions about how best to bring up your children, this is a dangerous sign. You should think very carefully about the alternatives: counselling, involving child psychologists, mediation, collaboration, and negotiation.

A lawyer can help, at least to begin with. So often the parents are so personally involved, thinking as an individual rather than as a co-parent, that they need the objective, pragmatic approach of a specialist children's lawyer, or a mediator, or an advisor. The lawyer will tell you whether you are behaving in a way that is objectively beneficial for the child. You can get this advice within an hour, and you will have the alternative of seeing what your other options are.

Needless to say, you should never resort to litigation without first taking clear legal advice as to the merits of your case and the cost-proportionality of the litigation you may be entering into. You also need to weigh up the potential damage to the dynamics of the family. What will the future be like if, every time there is disagreement about what is in the best interests of a child, you look to a third party – to a judge – to make a decision for you?

Prepare for frustration and delay

As public funding is being substantially reduced for individuals seeking to pursue claims concerning their children through the courts, more and more people are going to act in person – i.e., represent themselves before the court without any legal assistance to prepare them for going before the judge. If you are one of them, be prepared. The court case lists are going to be very full, and therefore it's going to get much harder for your case to be heard. Delays are going to be inevitable. For this reason, courts are going to be referring people to Separated Parents Information Programmes (SPIPs) and Mediation Information and Assessment Meetings (MIAMs) in order to consider alternative approaches to the confrontational litigious approach. (Information about both those things follows shortly.) They will encourage consensual approaches and mediation and a more costs-proportionate and time-proportionate way. They will be asking people to get real and get talking. Ultimately, communication is the only answer.

Putting your nose through the court door

If you are seeking a structure for dealing with the practical issues arising out of the parenting of your children following separation, the starting point lies in the four Orders that a court can make for children if the parents are unable to make their own arrangements. Those four Orders are:

- Residence
- Contact
- Specific Issue
- Prohibited Steps

Please note: anyone talking about 'custody' or 'care and control' is using seriously out-of-date legal language.

Please note also: courts are generally reluctant to intervene in cases where children are involved, preferring parents to find their own solutions. That is why Mediation Information and Assessment Meetings have to be considered before issuing or processing proceedings, and why courts insist that parents attend Separated Parents Information Programmes (SPIPS).

The Government is removing public funding to parents wanting to bring proceedings about their children in the vast majority of cases.

Nevertheless, sometimes it is necessary to bring an application before the court to show that you will not be brow-beaten against your attempt to do what is in your child's best interests, or that you will not allow your partner's inactivity to frustrate action that you believe is in your child's best interests.

There is a whole checklist that can be looked at in assessing what amounts to a child's best interests:

- The child's ascertainable wishes and feelings (considered in light of their age and understanding)
- The child's physical, emotional and educational needs
- The likely effect on the child of any change in their circumstances
- The child's age, sex, background and any characteristics the court considers relevant
- Any harm that the child has suffered or is at risk of suffering
- How capable each of the child's parents, and any other person in relation to whom the court considers the question to be relevant, is of meeting the child's needs

Residence

The way things are (the status quo) is very powerful when it comes to making decisions about children's best interests. Sometimes there is clearly one parent who has primary care of the children and one who has important but nevertheless secondary care. But it is becoming much more common for care of the children to be shared, and for both parents to have a roughly equal amount of care.

However, if you have been living apart for some time, the childcare arrangements when you were living together may have changed. This again is very important when making decisions about the welfare of your children.

Where there is conflict over residence arrangements, the problem is often that of the parents and not that of the child. Remember:

- Children want their parents to agree and to avoid conflict
- Children frequently want to stay where they are
- Children want clarity over their position in their home and their living arrangements with their main carer
- Children want to see both their parents
- Children want a clear lead from both their parents

It is the children who have these rights. Parents who think they have rights just don't get it. Parents have responsibility to their children. And they are responsible for making sure their child is protected from conflict and given a clear lead by both parents. The children have the right to that. It's not their conflict.

Residence: 'I' doesn't matter

When looking at residence as at any other issue concerning

children in a separation, parents too often use the word 'I' at the beginning of every sentence. They think that they have the rights. 'I am entitled to see my child when I want.' 'I want to do what I want with my child.' Well no, it is not like that. Residence orders exist to establish two things:

- Status (whom a child lives with)
- How a child shares time between the two parents

There are three kinds of residence arrangements:

1. 'No residence'
2. Sole residence
3. Shared residence

In a 'No-Residence' Order, everyone agrees that there is no reason for an order and no order is made. The vast majority of cases are of this type.

In a Sole-Residence Order there has normally been a dispute about whom the child will live with and the court has had to make a decision naming one parent. This happens where the parents cannot reach an agreement.

In a Shared Residence Order, the court may make the order on its own but more commonly it's made because of an agreement between parents who wish to avoid a full court hearing, which could entail the risk that one or the other obtains a sole-residence order.

Shared residence gives both parents that sense of responsibility and status, even if the reality is that the time is not shared equally for practical or other reasons. The child may spend more time with one parent than the other, even if the arrangement is that of shared residence. Sometimes a Residence Order, whether sole or shared, can be as much about the status of the parents as it is about the fine-tuning of how time is divided between the parents. Having a residence order in their name, even if it is shared, gives them a feeling of status in society as a parent.

Case Example: Vera and Jim

Vera and Jim have one son, Brian. Both think Brian, who is nine, would be better off living with them. They go to court to dispute residence, each seeking a Sole Residence Order and offering generous contact of six nights every two weeks to the other. They both think it is very important to have a court order to protect their position at law. They also want Brian to fully understand that he resides with them as the main carer. The judge says: 'I can either make an order, having heard from you both at length, providing residence to one parent and contact to the other. Or perhaps you would consider a Shared Residence Order, on the basis that Brian spends time with each of you, which you can decide on, and you both have the status of a residence order.'

Jim and Vera take the hint and ask for a Shared Residence Order on the basis that Brian spends 8 nights in every two weeks with her and six nights with Jim.

In my practice, I try and get away from use of words such as 'residence' and 'contact', and instead talk about how the child shares time with both parents. It seems more neutral and more fluid, and less threatening to both parents. Bringing the legal terminology into discussions between parents can make the discussion seem like a legal argument when it should be a joint cooperative effort to decide on what is best for one's children.

The sharing of time is often very difficult even with good will on both sides. This is why the sharing of residence and the sharing of time should be a jointly held decision. That means that it also makes sense for the court not to make an order where the parents are working well together. If one or both of the parents unfortunately believe there is a need for some kind of formal recognition of their role as a parent (their status), or for the precise sharing of time to be defined, then Shared Residence may be the way forward.

What will the children say?

Children have a say in their parenting and whom they live with – it is after all their welfare that is paramount and not that of their parents. It is important to give the children an opportunity to have a say.

But it is also important not to let the child decide on their own: it's better to listen to the child but then try and keep the decision with the parents. The emphasis on what weight should be applied to what the child says can vary with age. The older the child is, the more one has to take account of their views. Then the parents can make informed decisions as parents in their child's best interests, and the child can also feel listened to.

Children under 10

Before children reach the age of 10, parents really ought to take responsibility and reach their own conclusions, avoiding the conflict that is potentially so damaging for children. While professionals do sometimes make enquiries of the children and check out the options available for them, the court will try to promote an agreed way forward wherever possible. This does not mean involving the children as long as the parents agree to cooperate and work together. Only where there is parental conflict as to the best way forward will the court consider ascertaining the child's thoughts and wishes. This doesn't mean that the child makes the decision. Their wishes help inform the judge as to how he makes his decision – which the parents have placed in his hands.

Children 11 and over

Very often children aged 10 and over are consulted about their wishes, even if their wishes are not followed to the letter. Their view carries great weight depending on their maturity. Children aged 12 to 14 are very often capable of voting with their feet, and the court will give their wishes a lot of time if their parents are unable to agree on the arrangements. If your children are giving their views, you too should pay good attention to them.

Contact orders

Children all want to stay in touch with their extended families – their aunts and uncles, cousins, grandparents and friendship circles. They do not wish to be excluded as a result of their parents' separation. Unless there is a real risk of harm, both parents should try to make sure contact happens. The contacts should be both direct (face-to-face) and indirect (texts, emails, Skype, telephone calls, letters).

In every court decision regarding contact, the first principle is that the children's needs come first. To deny a child contact with another parent is something that that child lives with for the rest of their life. Doctors say that when a person has their leg amputated, they have a phantom pain in the leg which causes immense discomfort. To remove one parent from a child's world is equivalent to such an amputation; the child is subject to 'phantom pains', and they cannot easily share their pain with the parent with whom they continue to live. The courts recognise that for a child's wellbeing, they should be given every opportunity to remain in contact with both parents and both parents' extended families.

A contact order provides for when and where a child has direct contact or indirect contact with the parent with whom they do not live. The direct contact may take the form of a visit during the day, staying overnight, or holiday contact. Contact is sometimes also assisted by supervision. That means that the child is with the parent with whom they don't live but there is always someone else present. This can be ordered (or agreed) for a number of reasons:

- The parent with whom the child lives does not trust their partner
- The parent with whom the child lives will only agree to start contact on this basis
- The parent seeking contact recognises a need for help and guidance with the children at some stage

The supervision is normally provided by family members but can also be provided by friends or at contact centres. I would always encourage supervised contact to be part of the transition to unsupervised.

Sometimes in order to break the ice and enable contact to take place, when using the court process, parents are encouraged to use Contact Centres. However, Contact Centres are a transient step in terms of contact, and really should be used for a minimum period of time and used as a means to extend the contact between a parent and a child.

Contact: 'I' doesn't matter

When looking at the issue of contact, as at that of residence, parents too often use the word 'I' at the beginning of every sentence. 'I want to see the children.' 'It is not fair that I am held back from seeing them.' 'I know what's in her best interests and that is to have contact with me.' 'Why should I be refused contact as and when I want on these very reasonable dates and proposals?'

Complaints like these – however understandable – completely miss the point:

Contact is for the benefit of the child. It is not for the benefit of the parent.

Painful as it may be, you must get this idea into your head and let it guide all your thinking on the subject of contact. Once you get the priority right, it is easier to find a pattern of contact that can work best for the children. Your number-one aim should be to ensure that they have a clear, positive and constructive lead from both parents on the question of contact, rather than being immersed in conflict.

But beware. As a parent, do not put your new partner's interests ahead of your children's interests. Your new partner came into your life after the children, and the children come first in every decision regarding contact. Your new partner must fit around them and their needs.

Take your time, even if you and your partner are keen for your new partner to meet your children. You can make it possible to have better-quality contact between the children and your new partner if you get the timing right.

Where the court can help

The court can be helpful in dealing with contact issues. It can try to educate you in how best to see things from the perspective of the child, and ensure that you act for the benefit of the child, by providing Separated Parents Information Programmes (SPIPs), or giving guidance in the court environment.

Separated Parents Information Programmes

Separated Parents Information Programmes take place away from the court. They are often run by highly qualified mediators. Parents attend not as couples but as individuals and the groups are normally made up of six or more parents from different backgrounds. After a brief introduction and group discussion, a video is shown talking about the experience of children placed in the middle of parental conflict. And the information programme explores the impact of parents' behaviour on children. They are an educational hoop that you may have to go through before you can ask the court to deal with a court case involving children. This process is similar to the Mediation Information and Assessment Meeting (MIAM).

Mediation Information and Assessment Meetings

At a MIAM, your eligibility for public funding (legal aid) is assessed, as you can sometimes receive legal aid if you attend mediation. The MIAM explains the various processes available to you following separation, including mediation, and then describes mediation to you emphasising the impartiality of the mediator and the role of the mediator in helping you and your partner find your own solution to your own problems. It also assesses your suitability for mediation and establishes your willingness (or otherwise) to attend.

But very often there is not that much that the court can do, other than set out specifics in an order. Courts can be fairly toothless, for instance, when it comes to enforcing an order for contact. They cannot ensure that the points of collection and of return are treated sensitively by the parents, for this is the most common time of great difficulty on a contact visit. The conflict between parents and lack of communication come to the fore when collecting and delivering the children, because this is often the only time that separated parents come into contact with each other. You can avoid this often tragic problem by staying in touch with each other. Arrange to meet or talk on the telephone to discuss the children and the children's needs at times other than collection and return on contact visits.

The courts will try and encourage the sharing of festive days. For example, alternating Christmas and Boxing Day, or Christmas and Boxing Day and New Year's Eve and New Year's Day, or Christmas and Boxing Day and Easter weekend. But these periods, particularly Christmas, can be a time of immense stress. They are stressful for families where the parents are still living together, and even harder when a separation has taken place. You both need to work hard for the benefit of the children to make sure that you agree on the arrangements. You both need to feel fully involved in the plans, and to make arrangements that you agree are equally fair – or unfair.

Children's needs evolve

In the early years

Contact arrangements for young children depend on the child's age. To start with, when a child is very young, the contact can be little and often, to enable the child to bond with both parents and feel the benefit of a secure relationship with both parents while still very young. As the child becomes older, passing from, say, the age of one to the age of five, contact can be less frequent and for longer periods, extending to weekends or a night, or simply lengthy daytime visiting contact returning home at night to the parent with whom they live. This is because your children need to have regular frequent contact, so that they bond with both parents, particularly the parent whom they do not live with, and because they can keep their attention span while at the same time knowing they will return to the stability and security of their home.

Early school years

As children pass through infant school and junior school, they need to share time with both parents. This should provide an environment which helps them to benefit maximally from school.

So much happens to a child in the formative years from five to adolescence. To start with, in the early years, it's all about trying to encourage your child to feel good about themselves and feel able to develop their talents and be recognised for them. The last thing they need is to blame themselves for an adult's problem. The first thing they need is good contact – direct and indirect – with the parent they don't live with. They need to get a feel-good factor from both their parents.

Secondary school

By the time the children are approaching or attending secondary school and the closer adolescence approaches, the harder it is for them to deal with their emotions or be objective. That's why they see life in such stark, uncompromising terms. And the more they need to be involved in deciding how contact could work better for them.

Once a child is well established in secondary school, children focus much more on their friends and social life, and on establishing their independence. That means that parents need to work more around the child's needs and offer greater flexibility and support in their contact arrangements. This age group, while it tries to find its own independent way, still needs full involvement by both parents even if it is harder to provide. That's where listening to their views on how contact could be better becomes increasingly important.

Normally a good pattern of contact can be swiftly established, which can work provided the children's friendship circles and personal needs are protected, and the children are given their own time with each parent to enjoy.

Holidays

The approach to holidays varies from the standard pattern of contact that exists in term-time. Much often depends on the pragmatic needs of the caring parent to go to work, or their working hours, and how best to ensure that the children benefit from good care during long periods away from school. It's also a first-class opportunity for the parent with whom the child does not live to use their holiday time to provide (A) real benefit to the other parent and (B) quality involvement in the children's lives. This is one of the best ways to really make a difference to the other parent. The ultimate beneficiary of that is always the child – which should be reason enough for you to make a special effort to do it.

Specific Issue Orders

You can apply to the court for an order which relates to a specific issue, such as which school your child should go to, whether it is reasonable to move with your child to another part of the country or indeed to another country (also called 'removal from jurisdiction'). Specific Issue Orders normally involve significant issues and not relatively minor matters such as what food a child should be allowed to eat or what sports they are allowed to play. They can also include decisions on health when no agreement is reached.

Prohibited Steps Orders

By the same token, if you get wind of a plan to move school, or a plan to move location within the country or outside the country, you can apply to the court for a Prohibited Steps Order.

If the issue is highly significant when viewed from the outside looking in, rather than the inside looking out, then frequently help may be needed from an aide to the court in the form of a CAFCASS Officer (Children and Family Court Advisory and Support Service), a highly specialised social worker who specialises in assisting the court in decisions it makes with regard to children.

Specific Issue Orders and Prohibited Steps Orders are really two sides of the same coin.

Case example: Christina and Rob

Christina wishes to return to Canada, her country of birth, with Sam, her seven-year-old son. Rob, who is English, believes that Sam would be better off remaining in his local environment and school, and with his extended family and friends in Kent. Christina has told Rob that she intends to go to Canada anyway and Rob is concerned that she might just up and leave with Sam. Rob applies to the court to prohibit her from doing this.

The case then turns into a full-blown residence case. Should Sam live with Christina in Canada or Rob in Kent? The judge wants enquiries to be made and instructs a CAFCASS Officer to prepare a report after meeting with the family and make such enquiries as they think appropriate. This case presents such extreme choices and such high emotion where people would sacrifice almost anything to have their own way. Christina's motive is all-important – as is Sam's need to have a good relationship with both his parents. How do you decide? I suppose that's why we have judges.

The bottom line

Children do have a voice. Their voice needs to be heard. They don't, however, need to be the decision-maker. That rests with the parents, taking account of their children's voice. When two people have children, they really have got to sort out between them as parents the arrangements for their children. If they don't, they will fail in their responsibility to facilitate their children's right to expect good parenting decisions from them.

Welfare Check List

Section 1 of the Children Act 1989 requires the court to take into account the following when making decisions about children – and you should, too.

- The ascertainable wishes and feelings of the child concerned (considered in the light of the child's age and understanding)
- The child's physical, emotional and educational needs
- The likely effect on the child of any change in the child's circumstances
- The child's age, sex, background and any characteristics of the child the court considers relevant
- Any harm which the child has suffered or is at risk of suffering
- How capable each of the child's parents, and any other person in relation to whom the court considers the question to be relevant, is of meeting the child's needs

CHAPTER SEVEN

How Do I Get Divorced?

If your marriage has broken down, and there is no chance of your getting back together again, it really is not difficult to get divorced. The paperwork is designed to be easy for anyone to prepare. This chapter takes you through the procedures step by step.

Before dealing with the issue of divorce proceedings, there are a couple of practical things you need to take into account.

Which country am I getting divorced in – and why?

Some people have the right to issue divorce proceedings either in England and Wales or in another country. If you are among them, you may have good reason to issue your divorce proceedings in that other country. It could be that that is where the children live, or because you believe you would get a more advantageous financial settlement if the proceedings took place in another country. In the current world of global living too often it is an option that is ignored at considerable cost.

If you wish to issue proceedings in England and Wales, in which court are you going to issue your proceedings? Your local court, the court that your partner lives locally to, or a central court? The law is the same, but the practical implications of having proceedings going on at the other end of the country can be real and very difficult. Think about it carefully and take legal advice if you feel you need help.

What will be my grounds for getting divorced?

I think the process available for divorce is best understood if you realise that divorce does not need to be contentious. This country's laws often make it contentious, even when there is no good reason for that to happen. For over 40 years various governments have refused to make 'no fault' divorce available when less than two years' separation has taken place. The result is that if you want to get divorced before the two year period of separation elapses, you have to show that your partner has been at fault, insofar as they have committed adultery or behaved unreasonably. If you have lived apart for two years, in order to get a divorce you need your partner's consent. That consent is often given, but it cannot be assumed.

Law books tell you that in order to obtain a divorce, you have to show that your marriage has irretrievably broken down and that there is no prospect of reconciliation. The fact that your marriage has broken down needs to be evidenced, to use the legal term, in one of five ways:

1. Adultery
2. Unreasonable behaviour
3. Two years' separation with consent
4. Desertion
5. Five years' separation where there is no consent

The best way to look at the options is in reverse order.

Five years' separation where there is no consent

If your partner withholds consent to a divorce, in some circumstances you have to wait for five years' separation before you can legally show evidence of the irretrievable breakdown of the marriage. That means you would have to have lived separate and apart in different homes for five years. This way to divorce is fairly rare, as usually separating couples are able to agree other evidence to support the irretrievable breakdown of their marriage, and those proceedings can be issued without waiting the full five years. If you want to divorce, do try working with your partner to agree the issue of divorce proceedings and the basis on which the proceedings are issued. This enables you to avoid having to divorce based on this backstop scenario.

Usually, the main reason for using five years' separation as the basis of divorce is that one party wishes to make it impossible for the other party to remarry, or uses the stalling of the divorce to try and negotiate a bigger financial settlement. Often people agree to a divorce after two years' separation by consent, but increasingly people agree to be divorced for adultery or unreasonable behaviour in order to speed the process.

What should you do to avoid having to wait five years?

Case example: Jim and Sally

Jim and Sally were married and had two young children. Jim had an affair with Janice, who became pregnant. Jim wanted to divorce Sally in order to be able to marry Janice, who was pregnant with Jim's child. Sally had no wish for Jim to leave the marriage and believed that his relationship with Janice would fizzle out. Sally therefore refused to divorce, evidencing either Jim's adultery or Jim's unreasonable behaviour.

What did Jim do? He had two choices. He could either try to divorce Sally for her unreasonable behaviour, saying that she failed to show him affection and was verbally abusive towards him and rude to his family, while also exaggerating her behaviour in order to pressure her into a divorce. Or he could work with Sally to try and encourage her to contemplate a divorce in a reasonable timescale to meet his needs, as he was now living with Janice.

First Choice

Jim chose to press the divorce. He issued proceedings, which Sally made clear she would defend. Jim's lawyer told him it might cost £10,000 to £15,000 to pursue the divorce and he might not succeed. Jim's lawyer also told him that to press for a divorce in a non-consensual manner might alienate Sally for good and make his relationship with the children harder. Jim pressed on nevertheless. Eventually, Jim dropped the proceedings. But Sally determined not to allow him to have a divorce for his adultery or his unreasonable behaviour, not even after two years, and determined to make him wait for five years, when Jim ultimately issued divorce proceedings.

Second Choice

Jim spoke with Sally. Jim encouraged Sally to reconsider the position when the dust had settled in six or nine months' time. Jim understood that Sally did not want to facilitate his swift remarriage to Janice, even if Janice was pregnant. Jim made it clear that he would always be willing to pay for the issue of divorce proceedings against him, evidencing his adultery or his unreasonable behaviour, but at the very least he would expect to be divorced after two years' separation by consent. Sally said she would divorce Jim by consent after two years, and earlier if her life had adjusted in the meantime, as long as Jim paid her legal fees.

Desertion

To evidence desertion as the reason for the breakdown of the marriage is extremely rare. It is so rare, in fact, that I am not going to deal with it in any detail. It is enough to say simply that if you desert your partner for two years, which is the requirement, then probably after about two months you have behaved sufficiently unreasonably for divorce proceedings to have been issued earlier.

Two years' separation by consent

To obtain a divorce evidencing that you have lived apart for two years, you have to show that you have lived separate and apart for the whole of the two-year period. That usually, but not always, means living in separate homes, not under the same roof. As long as your partner consents to the divorce, this is a useful ground for divorce, as it carries no fault. It is a suitable basis for divorce where it has taken some time for the parties to decide to get divorced, even though they have been separated for longer. It is also a useful basis where one party has no wish to point the finger of fault at the other. And it is often kinder than waiting for a full five-year period of separation, as waiting that long to divorce can be damaging for both parties. Waiting beyond two years for a divorce means that your partner can remain stuck in a rut, unable and unwilling to be moved on through the grieving process. You find yourself waiting the full five years for the first time that you can issue divorce proceedings in an unimpeded way. This is normally because of your initial feeling of guilt that the marriage has broken down, and your wish to avoid conflict by issuing proceedings earlier. Ultimately, neither partner really benefits from the longer wait.

Unreasonable behaviour

Issuing divorce proceedings that evidence unreasonable behaviour is not always as bad as it sounds. What happens is the person bringing the divorce proceedings has to set out in a statement various areas of behaviour which they believe their partner has displayed towards them, which means that it is unreasonable for them to be expected to live with their partner.

The threshold of achieving unreasonable behaviour these days is very low. That is because nobody really approves of the need for fault-based divorce. Therefore normally it is sufficient for the statement to read along these lines:

- The partner is jealous and possessive
- The partner is rude and disrespectful about you in the presence of family and friends
- The partner fails to show you love and affection
- The partner behaved badly on various occasions through drink or over-exuberance
- The partner was aggressive or threatening

Generally speaking, it is best to exclude any reference to the partner's behaviour towards the children in the statement of case of an unreasonable behaviour petition, as it simply serves to inflame feelings. The particulars can be watered down in many circumstances to be acceptable to both parties.

In fact, if the person receiving the petition does not like the particulars, they can even write to the court and say that they are not defending the divorce, even though they believe the statement in support of the petition is in part exaggerated and in part untrue.

Adultery

The statement of case of an adultery petition has to say that the partner committed adultery with a third party, whose name you do not have to state and whose name is best not to state, from a certain date and in a certain town or area. The adultery is best referred to in a petition when the adultery has taken place in the last six months and where it is admitted. Otherwise, it is better to use it as a potential element in support of your unreasonable behaviour Petition.

Minimising the pain

If you can recognise that it is only right, where your marriage has broken down, for divorce proceedings to be able to take place in a non-contentious manner after a reasonable period for adjustment, you should be able to deal with the practicalities of divorce in a manner that avoids conflict.

Let's assume that you decide to proceed with divorce without waiting for two years to elapse. How can you do so in a positive way?

Case example: Angela and John

Angela wanted to divorce John for his unreasonable behaviour. In particular she felt that John lived life as a single man, away from the family; he did not provide her with love and affection; and he did not give enough attention to the children. He worked too hard and had a quick temper. John thought that the marriage had broken down some time before and that Angela had pushed him away from the family and made him feel unwelcome in his own home. He wanted to be thoroughly involved in the children's lives and felt that any reference to the children in the statement of case of unreasonable behaviour would adversely affect his future options with the children. John and Angela agreed that the particulars of unreasonable behaviour could say that:

- He lived life as a single man

- He put too much energy into his work and not enough into his family life
- He failed to show Angela love and affection

But they specifically agreed that there would be no reference to John's behaviour towards the children, and John found it acceptable to allow the petition to proceed on an undefended basis in that way.

It is always much easier if you both decide that it doesn't matter who divorces whom. If you don't care whether you are the one doing the divorcing or the one who is being divorced, you can help your partner divorce you. Not only will this speed things up, but it will also make it easier to have a relatively painless and conflict-free divorce. You will both benefit and so will your children. And no divorce lawyers will profit unduly.

The divorce process itself

In order to get divorced, you have to obtain a document called a Divorce Petition and complete it and file it with the court. That means finding your local County Court and giving them the signed Divorce Petition and copy, and the court then arranges to serve the Divorce Petition on your partner. The court will give you a blank Divorce Petition to complete. Otherwise, you can obtain one off the internet.

Before you issue the Divorce Petition, you will need:

- Your Marriage Certificate or a Certified Copy (the green one)
- A completed Statement of Arrangements for the Children, if there are children of the family (see below)
- The court fee (currently £410)

You will also need to provide certain details:

- The place of your marriage and your names at the time of the marriage (these need to be identical to those on your Marriage Certificate even if they are spelt wrong!)
- Your and your partner's date of birth
- Your and your partner's occupation
- The address at which you and your partner last lived together

You also need to confirm that the court has jurisdiction to deal with your divorce – normally because you and your partner are both habitually resident in England and Wales, or that either of you are domiciled in England and Wales. If you cannot show the court that you have jurisdiction or are domiciled in this country, then the court may reject your petition and tell you that you have to issue your divorce proceedings in another country.

You need to set out your wish to have a divorce and then indicate that you have grounds for divorce on the basis the marriage has broken down irretrievably, and then indicate which facts you rely on to support your application, be it adultery, unreasonable behaviour, desertion, two years' separation with consent, or five years' separation where there is no consent.

You need to detail the children's names, gender, date of birth. And you need to confirm your address for service of papers by the court, and your partner's address for service of papers by the court.

On the Divorce Petition the person bringing the divorce is called the Petitioner and the person receiving the divorce is called the Respondent (as they have to respond to the petition). The court staff will help you with any detail.

That just leaves the Statement of Case, which is the hardest part of the petition. How should you complete that? Use the information above about grounds for divorce as the basis, then write your statement with these points in mind.

Grounds for divorce: adultery

If adultery has taken place, then details of the adultery can be given to your partner to enable them to divorce you without naming the person with whom you committed adultery. When writing about the particulars of any adultery, simply state in the Statement of Case: 'the adultery took place on or around [a certain date] at or about [a certain place] with an unnamed third party'.

An adultery Petition would be questioned if someone condoned the adultery by living with their partner for six months after they knew that the last occasion of adultery took place. If this is the case with you, consider changing to the next particulars, namely unreasonable behaviour.

Alternatively, you can help your partner draw up particulars of your unreasonable behaviour during the marriage, or you could divorce your partner for their unreasonable behaviour during the marriage.

Grounds for divorce: unreasonable behaviour

This is more complicated than the Statement of Case in respect of adultery. It can also cause greater offence because not everybody accepts the criticisms of their former partner as being accurate. But the respondent can always write to the court saying that 'although they are not defending the divorce, they consider the particulars of unreasonable behaviour contained in the petition to be exaggerated and/or untrue'.

When drafting the statement of case to show unreasonable behaviour, it is best to do a general introductory paragraph saying, in non-contentious terms, what it is about your partner's character that you have found difficult to live with. Then, in about three or four paragraphs, specify each of those types of behaviour. It is useful also to add at the end of the particulars a last sentence which says: 'Further details can and will be provided in the event the Petition is defended'.

Try to include a date of the example of unreasonable behaviour in the Statement of Case within the petition. You will find this helpful later when filing your statement in support of the petition.

A typical Statement of Case for unreasonable behaviour might read:

> The Respondent is a person who is jealous and possessive, focuses on their work to the exclusion of the family, and has chosen to live life as a single person, and failed to show the Petitioner love and affection.
> The Respondent frequently works until 8 o'clock in the evening, returning from work unable to contribute to domestic family requirements, leaving the Petitioner to take on too much responsibility for the family's wellbeing and domestic chores.
> The Respondent is jealous and possessive of the Petitioner and is critical of the Petitioner in the presence of her friends and family.
> The Respondent chooses to live life as a single person, preferring to attend football matches and sporting occasions alone rather than spend time with the family as a whole, the last occasions being on 28th February 2013 when he went to a local football match.
> The Respondent fails to show the Petitioner love and affection.

The particulars do not need to detail the most extreme behaviour of the marriage. The Respondent will probably not accept them as accurate, and may well see them as being inflammatory. Try to agree the particulars of unreasonable behaviour with your partner before you file the petition with the court, so that you can make it into a document that your partner will allow to go through the court without defending the petition itself.

The main trick is to leave the children out when drafting the statement of case. Try not to put in disputed childcare issues. Focus on the relationship between the two adults and not on your spouse's parenting abilities. That is far less contentious.

The reason for this is simple: no partner is going to wish to accept their partner's subjective view that they are a bad parent, or a parent with poor parenting skills, or that they do not care for their children. They will see such a statement as a threat to their good intentions and sense of wellbeing, and will be concerned that the phraseology could be transmitted to the children at the time of the divorce proceedings, or later on in life, or generally used against them.

Case example: William and Catherine

Catherine had said she would give a statement claiming that William had been violent towards her, and hit her and the children during the course of their marriage. William agreed with Catherine that he would accept a petition from her but only if it did not contain those claims. Catherine ultimately decided, rather than set out the facts as she saw them, it would be wiser simply to allow the petition to proceed on the basis of an undefended divorce evidencing unreasonable behaviour, rather than her write an essay setting out her version of the facts of the marriage and the real reasons why the marriage had broken down. They agreed on the following wording:

> The Respondent is secretive with money and abusive, and shows the Petitioner no love and affection.

The Respondent is threatening and aggressive to the Petitioner, and shouted at the Petitioner, frightening her, on 5th November 2010.

The Respondent does not give the Petitioner details of his income or financial position in spite of the Petitioner's requests.

The Respondent is verbally abusive to the Petitioner in front of friends and family, calling her 'fat and lazy', and causing her intense embarrassment.

The Respondent has failed to show the Petitioner any love and affection since Christmas 2011, and intimate relations have ceased.

Further details can and will be provided in the event the Petition is defended.

You can see that Catherine's complaints about unreasonable behaviour are still pretty strong. But by choosing not to force through the claim of violence, she secured William's agreement to a statement that paints him in an unflattering light. Thus she avoided forcing William to defend the petition, which would have required an expensive and deeply unpleasant court battle.

Statement of Case for two years' separation by consent

In order to show that you have lived apart for two years, you simply have to state in the petition that 'the Petitioner and the Respondent have lived separate and apart since [date] and continue to do so and the Respondent consents to a decree of divorce'. It is at a later stage that you will be asked to provide details of the various addresses at which you have lived during the two-year period.

It is important to make sure your partner is going to consent to the Petition. When they receive the document from the court, they will be asked if they consent to the petition evidencing two years' separation, and it will be a waste of money if they were to indicate that they did not consent. You would have to go back to the court and file a petition on other grounds. And in any event, it is polite to involve your partner in the petition process and obtain their agreement to it.

Statement of Case for desertion

This is very simple. Just write:

'The Respondent deserted the Petitioner on [date] and has not returned since.'

Statement of Case for five years' separation without consent

Another very simple one:

'The Petitioner and the Respondent have lived separate and apart since [date] and continue to do so'.

A moment's prayer?

The most confusing part about the petition is on the final page where it sets out 'prayers'. Essentially prayers mean what you are asking for. The prayers say that you are applying for and asking for the marriage to be dissolved. There is also another prayer – request – if you are asking your partner to pay your fees arising from the divorce. These may be the court fees, or the court fees and any legal fees in connection with the divorce petition itself. The final prayer – application – is for a financial order. This list of financial claims includes maintenance, lump sum, property adjustment, pension and money for the children. The applications under 'prayers' can seem very threatening and can lead to misunderstanding. The general view is that it is wise to tick all the boxes in the financial application, so that in due course they can all be dealt with or dismissed. It is quite appropriate to do this as finances do need to be dealt with. Your position later on can be damaged if you do not tick all the boxes.

Obviously you do not need to tick the boxes in respect of the children if there are no children. These boxes still need ticking, even if you have reached a financial agreement with your partner. They set out the range of financial claims you are seeking as a result of filing the Divorce Petition and also deal with the question of costs. It is not unusual to proceed in a Petition with all the claims that are set out in this standard form, which can then be dismissed or withdrawn, therefore tick the boxes.

The specific claims are:

That the Petitioner may be granted the following Financial Orders:

(A) An order for maintenance pending suit/outcome

This exists where the party issuing the petition is asking for maintenance before the divorce is processed in order to meet their immediate needs. It is an unusual claim to make, as normally the parties come to some financial arrangement, and it is expensive to bring and can incur high fees. It really does make sense for both parties to come to arrangements that work for the family as a whole if at all possible.

(B) Periodical payments order

This is maintenance to be paid by the partner to the person bringing the petition. Often spouses overlook the fact that they are entitled to be maintained by their partner if there is a great disparity in their respective incomes. These maintenance claims can last for life, but are normally limited to remarriage, and can be limited to a shorter time span.

(C) Secured provision order

These orders are made where the maintenance tends not to be paid and therefore you will need to secure a bank account or savings to ensure that payment is made, whether the partner wishes to pay or not.

(D) Lump sum order

This is a capital sum dividing up the liquid assets of the parties.

(E) Property adjustment order

Who gets what property transferred into their name.

(F) Order under Section 24B, 25B or 25C of the Act of 1973/Paragraphs 15, 25 or 26 of Schedule 5 to the Act of 2004 (Pension Sharing/Attachment Order)

These tend to be Orders whereby there is a pension built up during the course of the marriage which is shared between the parties.

For the children:

(A) A periodical payments order

This is maintenance for a child where the Child Support Agency (CSA) are excluded, perhaps because the partner lives abroad or where there is very high income.

(B) A secured provision order

As above, if the maintenance payments cannot be relied upon, savings can be secured to ensure payment is made.

(C) A lump sum order

On occasion a lump sum order can be made for the benefit of the children.

(D) A property adjustment order

On occasion properties can be transferred to children during their minority or later on.

One thing you have to do now is discuss with your partner who is going to pay the petition court fees and any related legal fees. If you are going to pay them, or if you are confident that you are going to reach an informal arrangement, you can cross out that claim for costs altogether.

It is true that you should normally tick all the boxes for financial claims, because you want those claims dealt with and so will your partner. But if they are not dealt with, either you or your partner can later bring the claims before the court. The only situation in which you cannot bring the claims back before the court is if you have made no claims initially and you remarry having still not put the claims before the court.

Again, just to emphasise: only if you put in an application can the claims be dealt with by the court and resolved with finality. Do not forget that if you remarry before you make the claims, whether you are the petitioner or the respondent, you can lose the right to make a claim in divorce proceedings. Therefore you put your claims into the petition; and if you are the respondent, do not get remarried before you file your application for your own claims with the court.

Case example: Wilma and Graham

Wilma divorced Graham. She put no financial claims in her petition, although Graham and Wilma owned two houses that were in Graham's sole name and had lots of savings and both had a strong income. Wilma remarried before dealing with the finances. When she went to court to apply for her financial claims to deal with capital, property adjustment and pensions, the court told her it was too late. The only claims she had were on the properties on which she had her name, or on the bank accounts on which she had her name. She had no rights under the Matrimonial Causes Act. Wilma could not believe that she could not pursue her claims against Graham and lost out on a very substantial amount of money.

Case example: Sarah and Tony

Sarah issued divorce proceedings against Tony. She put in all the financial claims in her petition, as he owned numerous properties, had a large pension and a high income; she wished to pursue those claims against him. Tony had a new partner and remarried without filing his own application with the court to deal with the financial claims. Sarah was able to pursue her claims, but Tony, whose financial circumstances had also changed, was unable to pursue his claims against Sarah. Sarah had just won £3,000,000 on the National Lottery. Tony had had all his properties repossessed in respect of a large company debt that could not have been predicted. As a consequence, Sarah got to keep the whole of her money and Tony was not able to make a claim against it.

Case example: Anna and Jack

Anna and Jack both reached their own financial arrangements on the breakdown of their marriage. They did not want to obtain a court order dealing with their respective financial claims, although they both filed claims with the court that were never finalised. After they had reached their agreement, which was to split all their money equally, even though Anna had the four children of the family living with her, Jack suddenly realised that one of his investments had come good providing him with £500,000. Jack believed that he had finalised all Anna's claims by reaching an agreement with her, even though no court order had been made. Anna decided to pursue Jack through the courts for a share of the £500,000 and she succeeded in obtaining £250,000 because Jack had not asked the court to dismiss Anna's claims or made them final. There had been no clean break.

These three cases show how vitally important it is to settle all financial claims with finality. This should always be the aim.

Filing the petition

This is the act of putting your papers before the court once they are all complete. And you should try and go to court to file the papers in person. When you go to court, you go to a counter where you meet clerks who want to help you. They are busy, but able. It helps to talk face-to-face, and they can check the documents before accepting them and point out any glaring errors. You can correct the errors there and then without adding to your court fees by correcting them later.

It is really reassuring to know that the papers are with the court, and in order, and being processed. It is concrete evidence that things are moving on and you are making progress.

Sometimes papers get lost by the court. At least if you deliver them yourself, you know they are there and it cannot be said that they have been lost in the post. There is enough anxiety, stress and uncertainty when you are going through the divorce process, particularly when you are unfamiliar with courts and their processes. If you have hand-delivered the papers, you can then make it clear to your partner that they can expect to receive the papers within a week. Again: it is not at all intimidating to go to the court. Once you have filed the papers, you know you have really passed responsibility for them into the court process.

The Statement of Arrangements for the Children

At the same time as filing the petition, if you have children you are required to file a document called 'Statement of Arrangements for the Children'. The best way to deal with this is to sit down with your partner and fill it in together. It is much better if two parents can agree the proposed arrangements for the children, or at least identify the areas where they do not agree. If there are disagreements about the proposals for the children, whether it is their schooling, the amount of contact, or the financial support that is provided, then try and find a form of words you can agree on. You both are asked to comment on the document, and it is better if the document belongs to both of you.

If you cannot reach an agreement, the person who files the

petition is the person who should decide what goes in the form. It is then open to the Respondent to make their own observations on its contents when they file their Acknowledgment of Service (see below) after the Divorce Petition and Statement of Arrangements have been served on them. That is because the Statement of Arrangements is signed by the petitioner first: it is the petitioner's document setting out their view of the arrangements for the children. It is not the respondent's document. While that is the legal principle, the court will prefer to see a document that is approved by both parents if at all possible.

If you are the petitioner and therefore have responsibility for the content of the Statement of Arrangements for the children, you should put down your interpretation of the arrangements for them. It is then open to your partner to put their view to the court when they file the Acknowledgment of Service responding to the Petition and the Statement of Arrangements.

The Statement of Arrangements for the children is straightforward. You need to enter:

- The names of the children
- Whom they live with, and where
- The contact arrangements between the children and the parent with whom they do not live
- Who looks after the children on a day-to-day basis
- Where the children are at school

The Statement of Arrangements specifically provides the petitioner with an opportunity to say whether the arrangements set out are agreed, or if there is likely to be any change as a result of the divorce.

In addition, the form asks:

- If the children have any special educational needs

- If the children are in good health and have any special health needs
- If there are any special health needs, you need to set out briefly what they are and how they are provided
- Whether the children have been in the care of the local authority, in which case you need to give a brief indication of any proceedings relating to the children before the courts
- Whether the children are the subject of a Child Protection Plan
- Whether there are any children proceedings that are current, or have occurred in the past, relating to:
- Where they live or how they share their time with the parents
- Care or supervision
- Adoption or wardship
- You are required to attach copies of the Orders that you have
- Any maintenance arrangements that have been made with the Child Support Agency
- Whether there have been any proceedings for domestic violence or any non-molestation orders

Finally, you are asked to indicate, if you are not agreed as to the arrangements for the children, how you will try and resolve the disagreement that you have with your partner, be it through mediation, direct discussion or an application before the court. You are then required to sign the Statement of Arrangements and date it.

Case example: Jennifer and Gregory

Jennifer was divorcing Gregory. She thought the most appropriate contact arrangements for the children were that they see Gregory on alternate weekends from 6p.m. on Friday until 6p.m. on Sunday. Gregory thought that the appropriate contact arrangements for the children would be to see him each weekend from 4p.m. on Friday until 8p.m. on Saturday. Jennifer wanted to file the Statement of Arrangements indicating her proposed contact plans, and Gregory could not agree those in direct discussion with Jennifer.

Rather than delay filing the petition, Jennifer placed her proposals within the Statement of Arrangements, and when Gregory filed the Acknowledgment of Service he attached a letter to the court indicating that he did not agree the contact arrangements and proposed that contact take place weekly rather than fortnightly. The court accepted the petition and took the view that the arrangements for the children were adequate.

The Acknowledgment of Service

After the papers are filed with the court, usually it takes the court about a week to arrange for the petition and Statement of Arrangements to be forwarded to your partner at the address stated in the petition. Your partner is then given seven days to file an Acknowledgment of Service with the court. Often it takes longer than that in practice.

The person receiving the divorce papers should, however, try and file the Acknowledgment of Service in the time period specified and certainly return it within 21 days in order to avoid complications or the risk of having their legal position damaged by delay.

The Acknowledgment of Service is also a straightforward form. But it can contain more than just formal acknowledgement. It encourages you, for example, if you don't agree with any part of the Statement of Arrangements for the children, to set out how your views differ. You do this on a separate sheet of paper and annex it to the Acknowledgment of Service. If your partner is unhappy with the petition details, but accepts that the divorce should go ahead, they can always write to the court enclosing the Acknowledgment of Service, stating that they do not intend to defend the divorce, but reserve their position on the Statement of Case which they consider to be exaggerated or untrue.

Case example: Clare and Mark

Clare issued a petition stating that her husband Mark had been violent to her in the presence of the children, causing them great distress. Mark did not recall the incident that took place in that way and felt that he had been provoked by Clare into shouting at her in the presence of the children; he felt that they were equally responsible for the argument that took place and said also that there was no violence. He therefore thought that Clare's view was both exaggerated and untrue. That said, he accepted that the marriage had broken down, so he wrote a letter to the court stating that 'I consider the Statement of Case to be in part exaggerated and in part untrue. However, on the basis that I reserve my position with regard to any other proceedings relating to finances and the children, I will not defend the divorce, as I accept that the marriage has broken down irretrievably.' The court accepted the Acknowledgment of Service and allowed the petition to proceed on an undefended basis.

Both sides gain from this. There is no admission of 'guilt' on Mark's side, and Clare cannot claim that she 'won' unambiguously. But they both get the divorce that they feel is necessary.

It might take up to a month for the Acknowledgment of Service to be filed with the court and forwarded to the petitioner. If no Acknowledgment of Service has been received within a month, you should contact the court and ask if they have received it. If not, you should apply to the court for 'Directions' by writing a letter asking for the matter to be listed before the judge. In the normal course of events, however, you will receive the Acknowledgment of Service, and then it falls to you to go to the next stage.

The Statement in support of the Divorce and Application for Decree Nisi

This is an application for the certificate called 'Decree Nisi'. That means that the judge accepts that there are sufficient grounds to enable you to obtain a divorce. He or she will arrange for a date for the Decree Nisi to be pronounced in open court, a proceeding for which you do not need to attend at court. It is simply the occasion when the judge says you have proved you have grounds for divorce, and he or she provides a certificate saying that your divorce can proceed.

The intention of providing you this interim Certificate is to enable you to reconcile before applying for the final Certificate called a 'Decree Absolute', which you can do after a period of six weeks and one day has elapsed from the date of pronouncement of Decree Nisi.

The statement that you file with the court confirms that you still take the view that your marriage has broken down and that you wish to proceed with the petition. It gives you the opportunity to update your petition, if there are any key changes that are required – for example, changes of address. You file that statement with the court, along with the application for Decree Nisi. You can expect to be given a date for pronouncement of Decree Nisi within a month, and the date for it will then follow some three weeks later.

Generally speaking, there are no problems in filing these documents, though sometimes you are required to provide, as far as you are able, various addresses at which you and your partner may have lived (indicating that there has been two or five years' separation as the basis of your divorce). You are required to file the statement regardless of whether there have been any changes in the circumstances.

The issuing of the Decree Nisi is not the final divorce document. It is an interim holding position pending the application for Decree Absolute. This is the time when the court will also make any order for costs if a claim has been made. If you or your partner object to any claim for costs, you can attend at court and argue against the claim. You would normally hear from the court if that was your partner's intention, or the court might adjourn the question of costs, if it feels that both parties have not had the opportunity of being heard.

The court will at the same time also confirm whether it is satisfied with the arrangements for the children that you have set out in the Statement of Arrangements. Please bear in mind that even if the court says it is satisfied with the arrangements for the children, it does not mean that those arrangements cannot change at some point in the future.

Decree Absolute

This is the final Certificate of divorce. After the Decree Absolute has been pronounced, there is no going back – unless you remarry. You are entitled to apply for Decree Absolute six weeks and one day after pronouncement of Decree Nisi. You no longer have to pay a court fee for this. Your partner is entitled to apply for Decree Absolute, if you have not done so, three months after the six weeks and one day has elapsed, i.e. four and a half months from the date of the pronouncement of Decree Nisi. Often it is wise not to apply for Decree Absolute until financial issues have been finalised, particularly if a Pension Share Agreement has been entered into (see the next chapter). If this is the case, you should wait for 28 days after the Pension Sharing Order has been made.

It is quite realistic for divorce proceedings to be processed in four months, and certainly within six months. Where it takes longer, the delay is almost always a result of dispute and of lack of cooperation between the separating partners. Working together will save you not just time but money – and emotional distress.

A final word: three problems to avoid at all costs

- Having the papers returned because of some technical defect. In those circumstances, speak to the court and try again.
- If your partner fails to file the Acknowledgment of Service, that can lead to delay, and you have to prove service of the petition and related papers on your partner. Encourage your partner to file the Acknowledgment of Service indicating no intention to defend; or ask the court to arrange for personal service of the petition on your partner. Fill in the form called a Request for Personal Service by a court Bailiff. Provide a photograph and the relevant fee and the court will try to effect personal service of the petition paper on your partner, so that you can file your Statement in Support in the knowledge that the petition has been served.
- If the Acknowledgment of Service is returned indicating an intention to defend the petition, ask the court to list the matter for Directions without delay. This is a very rare event in practice. Write a letter to the court acknowledging that your partner intends to defend the petition and ask the court to list the matter for Directions so that you can press on with your divorce with the court's guidance.

CHAPTER EIGHT

Money Matters

Dealing with money issues arising out of the breakdown of your marriage does not necessarily need to be complicated or difficult. It all depends on what financial resources you have, and what the respective needs of the family are.

If you have no money, or if there are debts, the picture is clear if not necessarily very pleasant. Either you pay the debts or there is the threat of bankruptcy hanging over you. The first thing to do when dividing money is to make sure that you have the means to clear your debts if at all possible.

If you do have any money, then you need to look at what is the level of your assets. Are they sufficient to provide a home for one of you or – far more importantly – the children? If not, then the money is going to be divided in such a way as to provide for each of your respective needs without incurring the major expense of the purchase of a house or the retention of a house.

If there is enough money to meet the housing needs of a child living with a resident parent, then the next stage is to see if there is enough to also meet the housing needs of the other parent. The child will be staying with that parent, even if they do not live there but merely visit.

If there is more than enough money to meet two housing needs, then the basic needs are met, and the financial decision-making gets increasingly easier.

Over and above taking into account the needs and resources

of both parents and the children, you need to take into account:

- The adults' ages
- Length of the marriage
- Contributions made by each of the parties to the marriage
- What pension provision they have
- Whether there are any health issues

Money in detail

Your thinking about money will be made much easier if you put the vital points down on paper. The following checklists are a good starting point.

First of all, you need a summary of your capital – also known as a Summary of Assets. This is simply the value of everything you own as a family. You can determine it using this simple list identifying who owns what:

- Current value of your interest in the family home
- Current value of your interest in all other property
- Current value of your interest in personal assets
- Current value of your liabilities
- Current value of your interest in business assets
- Current value of your pension
- Current value of all your other assets
- Total value of your assets

Next you need a summary of your estimated income for the next 12 months. Calculate it using this list:

- Estimated net total of income from employment
- Estimated net total of income from self-employment or partnership

- Estimated net total of investment income
- Estimated State Benefit receipts
- Estimated net total of all other income
- Estimated total income for the next 12 months
- And estimated maintenance

The next thing you need is a summary of monthly expenditure. This is a much more complicated area, and mediators use a standard form to calculate it. You can download and print the form at the web address given in Further Reading at the end of this book, and you would be well advised to do so: it is an invaluable tool.

When you first look at the form, some of the lists may seem excessively detailed if you have never budgeted in this way. But the more closely you look at your finances the easier it will be to get the full picture. And the big picture is going to be very important in making decisions about money.

The summary includes property costs, financial costs, household expenditure, personal expenditure, car expenditure, leisure expenditure and children expenditure.

Analysing your expenditure is an interesting exercise. It is not difficult to put down a list of expenditure that you would like to be able to fund. What is important, however, is to put down a list of expenditure that is within your means.

It is also important to see whether the expenditure that you put down for your property and other items is comparable to the expenditure that your partner puts down. The housing cost is normally fairly straightforward, and there is enough of a historical record to give you a fairly clear and accurate indication of current and future costs.

The idea with financial costs, such as credit cards, loans, pension costs and life assurance, is that they are predominantly in your control. They are figures that you always aim to reduce where possible, while protecting your housing and capital needs. They are the area that requires most focus.

Expenditure on running a car is fairly predictable, as is the expenditure on household living expenditure, personal living expenses and leisure. It is in these areas that an element of comparison between households needs to be established, taking account of the combined income of the family. Never overlook the capacity to increase your income through making appropriate applications for tax credits and other state entitlements.

When analysing your capital options, having prepared your Schedule of Assets, always look to the amount of equity, excluding pensions. Combine that with your respective mortgage capacities, anticipating your income, including from maintenance and tax credits, and see if the combined figures are sufficient to provide housing for the children, while sharing time with each parent.

Financial decisions split naturally into three areas.

1. Maintenance
2. Pensions
3. Capital

I like to refer to these as three financial pots. It helps if you look at them both individually and as a whole when considering your financial options on divorce. Before you look at them, however, you need to have a clear understanding of what your assets are. And the best way to start is by filling in the forms given above.

Get ahead

The thing that often takes longest to establish in your schedule of assets is the cash equivalent transfer value of your pension or pensions. You should request this from the pension companies as early as possible. Having done that, draw together all your other assets:

- Bank accounts
- Savings accounts
- Stocks and shares
- Endowments
- Premium Bonds
- Other investments

Make a summary of your assets in a schedule of assets, using five columns:

1. Name of asset
2. Jointly owned
3. Owned by you
4. Owned by your partner
5. Notes about the asset

After each asset write down who owns what: whether the asset is held in joint names, in your sole name, or in your partner's sole name. If you have any observations on the asset, do a note alongside.

The preparation you've done so far sets out your own finances but not those of your partner. They must give you the same information to help you draw together a more complete picture of the family's finances. They too should draw together a schedule of assets in five columns.

Income, from all possible sources

You need to have in the back of your mind your eligibility for benefits, including housing benefit and tax credits and Child

Benefit, as it will be when you are living apart. This is in addition to your income from other sources, which is less likely to change. Add this to your income and make use of the summary of estimated income for the next 12 months to draw together your total income.

Expenses

You should also have a concept of your potential core expenses. Use the summary of expenditure to draw together your current and projected monthly expenditure. And don't stray far from present realities. Keep it real.

Assembling this information, even if some of it is guesswork, gives you the raw material to start looking at what the future could look like in financial terms, and at what your options are.

Pot Number One: Maintenance

There are two types of maintenance: for children and for a spouse.

Children: it starts with the CSA

The starting point, when dealing with maintenance for children, is to look at what the Child Support Agency (CSA) calculation amounts to. The CSA calculation is based on the income received by the parent with whom the child is not living. It is expressed as a percentage and takes into account the average number of nights that a child spends each week with each parent. At the moment, the calculation in basic terms is:

- 15 per cent of net income for 1 child
- 20 per cent of net income for 2 children
- 25 per cent of net income for 3 children or more

There are various discounts to this. In one, for example, the percentage is cut by 1/7 for every 52 nights in a year that the children stay with the paying partner. Another discount applies if the paying partner is responsible for other children too. It can all seem very complicated, but the CSA has a very accessible online calculator. You'll find the address for it in Further Reading at the end of this book.

Once that figure is determined, you have a starting point or a fall-back position for further discussion. For instance, you can use the CSA calculation as a base to discuss your respective resources and needs as a parent. You can also use it as a base to discuss other parenting issues, such as school trips, children's clothing, presents for the children, school fees, and one-off costs such as computers. You both need to plan your finances and to come up with a maintenance formula that is affordable for the payer and adequate for the recipient.

If your partner's income is very high, say above around £100,000 net a year, you can apply to the Court to top up the CSA calculation. But that happens only in a small percentage of cases.

And such applications are not normally necessary, as it is reasonable to expect parents to agree the way forward by planning and budgeting as parents – as if they were living together. You are both still parents, after all, and there is no need to let your financial anxiety spill over into the children's needs. If the arrangements can be discussed in a sensible co-parenting way, and the money is there, putting the children's interests first should be the natural first option for both of you.

Problems with payments

If arranging and getting payments is a problem, you can always involve the CSA and they will police the payments that are required and enforce the payments that are made.

Note, however, that different rules apply if one parent lives abroad. The CSA does not have the authority to enforce payments on parents who live abroad, so if there is no agreement about the level of maintenance, the parent living in this country has access to the court to obtain a maintenance order for the child. That maintenance order may well be based on a CSA calculation as a starting point.

If you are the one trying to get payments enforced, remember the old saying that a bird in the hand is worth two in the bush. It is better to have one payment that is agreed and transferred than no money because no agreement has been reached. That said, it is often possible to enforce payments abroad, but it can take time. And it can be an expensive process – so be careful before going down that route if a realistic compromise is available to you.

The whole rationale behind the CSA is to encourage parents to agree the level of maintenance for the children, and to use the CSA as a backstop only. That is why the calculation of the amount of maintenance has been kept to a simple percentage. And that is why the CSA is soon to apply a charge to anyone using its services. An agreement between parents is so much more constructive than a figure enforced by the CSA. It carries flexibility and trust, and it seems only appropriate that two parents agree the level of financial support needed for their child or children.

Maintenance for spouses: the two L's

The first decision here is deciding on the length of time that payments will be made, and it comes as a surprise to many separating adults to learn that spouses have claims against their partner for life. And even if the maintenance claims do not last for life, they can at least go on until remarriage.

But sometimes the maintenance claims can be dismissed immediately. For example:

- Where both parents have a similar earning capacity or income
- Where one person has received a greater proportion of capital or pension to offset maintenance
- Where the partner entitled to maintenance is cohabiting

Note, however, that it is unusual to dismiss maintenance claims where there are young children, other than by agreement. This is often dealt with by a nominal maintenance order, which leaves the door open to deal with any future change in circumstances and leaves the maintenance issue alive. This essentially means there can be no certainty or absolute clean break.

You can also look at restricting the period of payment of maintenance until the age of retirement, or to some shorter date, such as when the additional income is no longer needed to assist in the support of children. Much depends on the circumstances of each separation.

Apart from the length that the maintenance payments are to be made, the level of maintenance is the other major item to be decided upon. Agreeing on maintenance is often difficult, and there's no question that this can be a delicate balancing act.

Generally speaking, the level of maintenance takes account of both parents' incomes and the difference between them. It looks at the needs of both parents, after taking into account any child maintenance that is paid, and tries to provide a figure that leaves the paying person feeling both motivation to work and a reasonable reward for working. At the same time it aims at meeting the needs of the person receiving maintenance while encouraging them too to maximise their own earning capacity and use of benefits.

The level of maintenance rarely exceeds more than half the

net income of the payer, including any child maintenance being paid. It can often be calculated as a percentage of joint income, or indeed the overall income of the partner who is paying.

Points to consider

In negotiating the duration and level of maintenance, you may want to take account of:

- Your partner's prospects of remarrying
- Your wish for independence
- Whether you are protecting yourself against illness or loss of employment, particularly if you have young children

Many people like the idea of a clean break and financial independence. One person is often willing to buy out the other's maintenance claims in exchange for a bigger interest in the house or assets. This is a good idea if they can afford it. However, be careful before agreeing to this if you have young children or uncertain employment prospects.

There are orders given under Section 28(1A) of the Matrimonial Causes Act that ensure an absolute clean break from a certain date. Otherwise clean-break orders, or orders ending on a certain date, are open to extension and variation. This is particularly significant because you and your partner need to plan for the future. The paying partner will want to know when his obligations come to an end, so that he look at his options such as retirement with certainty. The person receiving maintenance will want to know at what date they have to establish financial independence and their own earning stream, without depending on the paying partner.

It is also very important to remember that spousal maintenance can always be varied and amended to go up or down, depending on any change in financial circumstances as time goes by.

Pot Number Two: Pensions

Pensions are usually built up over many years, and they are complex assets. They carry hidden values which are difficult for a lay person or a non-specialist lawyer to identify. An example of a hidden asset in a pension pot might be a Guaranteed Pension, or a Pension invested in business premises, or a private Self Invested Pension Policy (SIPP).

Before you can decide how best to divide the pension, you need to establish its true value. You should not baulk at obtaining an Actuarial (professional) Valuation of Pensions, particularly if the pension values appear to be over £150,000. Only when you know the value of the pension can you decide how best to divide it.

As a starting point, you should be looking to share the value of a pension pot built up during the period of marriage or cohabitation equally. You should also establish how the pension pot can be divided to provide for equal income on retirement, as the pot may need to be divided unequally to take account of different life expectancy.

Case example: Nicole and Gerry

Nicole is 50 and Gerry is 58. Gerry plans to retire at 65. He has a substantial pension and Nicole has none. Gerry will maintain Nicole until he retires. After that, his pension is to be split to provide them both with the same income for life. Nicole's life expectancy at the time of retirement could be eight years longer than Gerry's. In order to buy an annuity providing the same income, she will need a larger lump sum because she will need support from the pension fund for a longer time.

Much depends on how much of the pension was built up

during the marriage or cohabitation, and how much was built up before then. You can look to offset the value of a pension fund against liquid assets, or the equity in a property, but a pound in a pension does not have the same value as a pound in the bank or indeed a pound in a house.

Most people's views on pensions change during the course of their adult lives. If you offered an 18-year-old a pension pot of £1,000 or a pint of beer, they would take the beer. As you get older, the value of a pension pot has a greater value to you as a person. It's a common mistake to undervalue pensions, not least because they are so varied in their makeup. Some carry guarantees and some carry hidden assets. People generally prefer to have income (maintenance) in the moment or more capital to meet their immediate housing needs rather than plan for their future over the long term. That is why Financial Advisors can provide you with excellent advice which enables you to get a good overview as to planning your financial future in broad terms.

Pot Number Three: Capital

Normally the principal asset to be divided in some way or other, over and above the pension, is the family home. Right from the start you should assume you will have to downsize your house, and you will almost certainly need to finance two houses out of the equity in one house. Much depends on each of the two adults' respective abilities to meet mortgage payments.

Just to repeat: the housing needs of the children have first priority. After that the housing need of both parents to be able to offer the children a comparable home becomes relevant. So: after the children's housing needs have been met from the available resources with one parent, then one can try to ensure that there is enough to provide the children with adequate housing while sharing time with the other parent.

Most people like to divide the capital assets of a marriage once and for all, in a way that does not need to be revisited. But sometimes the assets are insufficient. In order to provide for the housing needs of the children where there isn't enough money to provide comparably comfortable housing for both parents, often the parent with whom the children spend most time may get more of the liquid assets to provide housing, while the other partner takes more of the 'future' money (e.g. pension) as an offset. Alternatively, the parent with the children may have more of the assets to provide housing until the children reach a certain age and be assisted in the provision of that housing by the other parent. One lends the other money (e.g. their share of the house) by way of what is known as a charge-back.

The charge-back is often expressed as a percentage of the house and enables the lender to pay off the mortgage that they cannot afford or put down a deposit on a new property when the timing fits the children's needs. That means that one parent keeps a continuing interest in a house occupied by the other. That partner turns into a bank, lending money, secured against the house, to their former partner. It often happens where there is not enough money to provide two homes, just one, and both parties want to have the opportunity of sharing the increased value in a retained home until a fixed event, such as remarriage, or the children finishing their education.

Essentially, once the debts are cleared, you are looking to house the children first, and then any spare money can be used to house the parent with whom the children do not live, but whom the children visit.

Dealing with the surplus

Once that division has taken place, the choices about how to invest the money are left with the parents.

If there is more money around after housing needs have been met, then you need to look at how it has been accumulated. Were assets built up before the marriage and brought into the marriage? Were assets accumulated after separation but before the divorce was finalised? Was money inherited? Is there money in an old family weekend cottage or family business? Only when you've identified all the different sources can you work out how to divide the assets most fairly, which also entails taking into account factors such as the length of the marriage, the two partners' ages and their health.

One major area of difficulty often comes in valuing the assets. It is difficult enough to value a house let alone a business or business shares. Often you need experts to assist you in getting to a clear valuation. Particularly tricky areas to watch for include:

- Interests in privately owned companies
- Share options
- Minority shareholdings
- Quasi-Partnerships
- Trust funds
- Inheritances
- Land with development value
- Payment of university fees
- Guaranteed and Protected Pensions

If any of these items carry a major weight in your case, or are causing substantial difference of opinion, then you need to take expert advice as to what your options are. Your lawyer cannot advise you on values with any real authority as he or she is not a Financial Advisor. You need to have confidence in your understanding of the finances and the value of the assets. If you have to pay an expert to gain that confidence, the money will be well spent.

You also need to consult a Financial Advisor in order to help you assess what your needs are going to be up to retirement and beyond retirement, and whether there are going to be sufficient funds for both adults to be supported up to and through retirement from the assets already built up within the marriage. The Financial Advisor can provide cash flow forecasts that are a good indicator of what is and what is not possible.

And finally…

Section 25 of the Matrimonial Causes Act (1973) requires the court to have regard to the following when dealing with financial matters – so you should, too.

- Needs
- Resources
- Age
- Children
- Health
- Contributions
- Standard of living
- Pension
- Length of marriage
- Fairness

But just because that is the approach taken by the law, it does not mean it is an exclusive list of what you consider in trying to find the solution to financial matters. Your combined thoughts as to the range of options have a great deal more flexibility and should be explored.

Postscript: What do you do if you are not married?

If you are not married, or if you are not planning to marry, the applicable laws are different from those that apply with married couples. The financial position on separation if you are not married is very different from that of divorce.

In a divorce, ultimately if no agreement is reached, the judge has an overriding discretion about how to proceed and divide the money. That is not the case if you are not married. However long you have lived together or however many children you have, the way finances are dealt with depends on what the house deeds say, what any trust document contains, and whose name the bank account and Premium Bonds are in. It is open to both live-together adults to reach their own decision as to the way forward. However, they need to record this clearly in writing. It is a constantly changing area of the law requiring review and advice.

So if you are not married and your relationship breaks down, your entitlement to bring claims in the same areas referred to above is as follows.

Maintenance

There is no 'spousal' maintenance payable from one adult to the other. There is only maintenance payable under the CSA, as referred to above, for a child. And exactly the same process applies for a child as applies within divorce.

Pension

Neither party has a claim against each other's pensions, and no Pension Sharing Order can be made.

Capital

Capital claims depends on the deeds to the property. If the deeds do not have your name in them, they do not protect you. Should this be the case for you, establish whether you have reached an agreement in a formal way by way of a Declaration of Trust or otherwise that records how your assets should be divided on separation. Essentially, if the deeds show that the property is in your sole name or your partner's sole name, that is the starting point in discussion of what should happen to that asset. If the deeds show that the property is held by you and your partner in joint names, that is the starting point. If the assets are not to be dealt with in that way, then you or your partner will have to establish that a Trust exists in the form of a Resulting Trust or a Constructive Trust. In both types of trust, there is clear evidence that although the deeds say one thing, the intention that you both had, or the financial contributions that you had both made, mean that the property should be held differently from the way the deeds state.

Resulting Trust

To establish a Resulting Trust, one has to show that a person whose name is not on the deeds has invested money in the property and as a result there is a presumption that that investment gives that investor an interest over and above what is stated in the deeds on that property. If this can be proved, a Resulting Trust exists.

Constructive Trust

A Constructive Trust exists if one person has acted to their detriment. A fairly common example is where one partner does substantial building works to a property, on an understanding that there was a common intention that the property, though stated in the deeds as belonging to the partner, was in practice to be held on different terms. However, different people have different recollections of what the 'common intention' was. You are much wiser to record what your plan is about ownership of the property and to keep that under constant review.

This is an area that is constantly under the scrutiny of Parliament and constantly the subject of expensive cases before the courts. Governments have been considering a change in this legislation for many years, as it leads to many anomalies and unfair outcomes, and gives the adults difficult imbalances of power when negotiating their way forward on separation.

Beware: proceedings under the Trust of Land and Trustees Appointment Act, which covers both types of trust, are extremely expensive. They take a long time to process and it is difficult to predict the outcome. The approach taken under the law carries little discretion, and one person's concept of fairness is very frequently at odds with their partner's. This can be the cause of enormous distress and anxiety.

The only answer is to clearly record your intention before the separation, and not to try and find out what the intention was after.

Children Act Proceedings

Where a child is yet to finish full-time education, the parent who has care of them can bring proceedings on their behalf for capital to meet housing costs, living needs, and one-off needs. This is done through the Children Act, and often an application under the Children Act is used to complement an application under the Trust of Land and Trustees Appointment Act. This can be the route, for example, to use a father's funds to meet the housing needs or educational school fees costs for his child where the parents have separated or do not live together.

By the way: Pre-Nuptials/Post-Nuptials/Trusts

If you do not want the uncertainty and lack of knowledge of what would happen on separation, then there is nothing to stop you before the marriage or during the course of the marriage from entering into a pre-nuptial agreement or a post-nuptial agreement, or entering into a Trust Fund making it quite clear what your intentions are if you separate or if the marriage breaks down.

A share of what's unfair

Overall, you are hoping to come out of your divorce with what you view as fair. But the trouble is that fairness is very much a subjective test and each person has a different view of what it means. Here is an idea that may seem alien but can actually work quite well in these discussions:

It is often easier to try and find a resolution that is equally unfair, rather than a resolution that is fair for both. Nobody wins financially when you split a family's income and capital between two homes rather than one. Everybody loses out. Therefore it's difficult to work towards a solution that seems fair, because both sides are suffering. And the only solution is try and balance the sense of unfairness in any financial solution that you reach.

The bottom line about the bottom line

With money (and indeed with everything else), do everything you can to minimise conflict. When dealing with issues and disputes that arise following the breakdown of a marriage, you should do all you can as separating partners to be constructive, positive, enthusiastic, energetic and innovative in your search for resolution.

CHAPTER NINE

Further Reading

At A Glance: Essential Tables For Financial Remedies (Class Legal, http://www.classlegal.com)

Dinosaurs Divorce: A Guide for Changing Families, Laurene Krasney-Brown and Mark Brown (Little, Brown Books for Young Readers)

Getting To Yes, Roger Fisher and William Ury (Random House Business)

Men Are From Mars, Women Are From Venus, John Gray (Harper Elements)

Rebuilding: When Your Relationship Ends, Dr Bruce Fisher and Dr Robert Alberti (Impact Publishers)

Second Chances: Men, Women and Children a Decade After Divorce, Judith S. Wallerstein and Sandra Blakeslee (Houghton Mifflin)

Separation and Divorce (Resolution, http://www.resolution.org.uk)

Surviving The Break-Up, Judith S. Wallerstein and Joan B Kelly (Basic Books)

Online Resources:

Child Maintenance Calculator
http://www.gov.uk/calculate-your-child-maintenance

Monthly Expenditure Calculator
http://www.mediationfirst.uk.com/PDFs/Budget_form.pdf

Downloadable Divorce Papers
http://www.divorce-forms.co.uk/